ArtScroll® Series

THE SCHOTTENSTEIN EDITION

סדר תשליך

THE INTERLINEAR TASHLICH

WITH INTERLINEAR TRANSLATION, COMMENTARY, AND OVERVIEW

Edited by
Rabbi Menachem Davis

Contributing Editors:
Rabbi Nosson Scherman
Rabbi Meir Zlotowitz
Rabbi Yaakov Blinder

Designed by
Rabbi Sheah Brander

First Impression . . . September 2025

Published and Distributed by
MESORAH PUBLICATIONS, Ltd.
313 Regina Avenue / Rahway, New Jersey 07065

Distributed in Europe by
LEHMANNS
Unit E, Viking Business Park
Rolling Mill Road
Jarrow, Tyne & Wear NE32 3DP
England

Distributed in Australia & New Zealand by
GOLDS WORLD OF JUDAICA
3-13 William Street
Balaclava, Melbourne 3183
Victoria Australia

Distributed in Israel by
SIFRIATI / A. GITLER — BOOKS
POB 2351
Bnei Brak 51122

Distributed in South Africa by
KOLLEL BOOKSHOP
Northfield Centre, 17 Northfield Avenue
Glenhazel 2192, Johannesburg, South Africa

THE ARTSCROLL® MESORAH SERIES
INTERLINEAR TASHLICH

ITEM CODE: ITASP
ISBN 10: 1-4226-4541-X / ISBN 13: 978-1-4226-4541-3 (paperback)

Typography by Compuscribe at ArtScroll Studios, Ltd.
313 Regina Avenue / Rahway, N.J. 07065 / (718) 921-9000

Printed in the United States of America

This volume is lovingly dedicated
in memory of our fathers

צבי בן יואל לאוב ז״ל
Mr. Harry Laub ז״ל
אברהם בן אהרן אלימלך גאלדפארב ז״ל
Mr. Arnold Goldfarb ז״ל

We grew up with the *zechus* of hearing our fathers daven for the *amud* as *baalei tefillah* for the Yamim Noraim. Between the two of them, they davened all of the *tefillos* on both Rosh Hashanah and Yom Kippur. As masters of both *nusach* and *niggun*, they were able to inspire their *kehillos* during the *Yemei HaDin* because their *tefillos* came from the heart.

Despite not having heard their davening in so many years, to this day their voices remain in our memories and continue to enhance and uplift our *tefillos*.

Through their *tefillos*, צבי בן יואל ז״ל and אברהם בן אהרן אלימלך ז״ל were *zocheh* to inspire hundreds if not thousands of people to draw close to Hashem.

May this *sefer* serve as an inspiration to others during the Yamim Noraim and be a *zechus* for our fathers' *neshamos*.

יהי זכרם ברוך

Meir Yoel and Susan Laub and Family

The text of the Interlinear Tashlich comes from the
Schottenstein Edition Interlinear Machzor for Rosh Hashanah,
dedicated by Jay and Jeanie Schottenstein

The Interlinear Machzor for Rosh Hashanah
is dedicated with love to our children,

Joseph Aaron and Lindsay Brooke
Jacob Meir, Jonah Philip, and Emma Blake

Jonathan Richard and Nicole Lauren
Winnie Simone, Teddi Isabella, and Allegra Giselle

Jeffrey Adam
Jerome Meir and Debbie

They represent the dreams of our past generations
and they bring pride to us every day.
They are the building blocks of our future.

The Rosh Hashanah Machzor reverberates
with the beauty of Judaism
across oceans and through the ages,
and with the goals, hopes, and
aspirations of our people.

May this volume bring joy, spirit, and inspiration
to families and communities
throughout the world.

Jay and Jeanie Schottenstein

An Overview / Depths of Repentance

I. Abraham's Victory

כְּשֶׁהָלַךְ אַבְרָהָם אָבִינוּ לַעֲקוֹד אֶת יִצְחָק בְּנוֹ הוֹלִיכוֹ הַשָּׂטָן בְּנָהָר עַד שֶׁבָּא עַד צַוָּארוֹ בַּמַּיִם. וְאָמַר אַבְרָהָם: "הוֹשִׁיעָה ה' כִּי בָאוּ מַיִם עַד נָפֶשׁ" וְנִיצוֹל.

When our forefather Abraham went to bind his son, Isaac [on the altar], Satan led him through a river until the water came up to his neck. Abraham said, 'Help, HASHEM, for water menaces our lives!' Then, he was saved! (*Tanchuma, Vayeira* 25).

Sons of Prophets

THE CUSTOM OF *TASHLICH* IS OBSERVED WHEREVER there are Jews. Sephardim and Ashkenazim, who had been separated from one another by continents and centuries, all observe *Tashlich*. Yet there is no mention of it in the Talmud, or the early Rishonim. Even in the *Shulchan Aruch*, it has the barest of mentions (*Rama, Orach Chaim* 583:2). The earliest printed reference to *Tashlich* is in *Maharil*, but he does not say who instituted the practice, only that it is a Jewish custom. *Tashlich* appears to be a manifestation of Israel's genius to devise ways of perfecting itself in the service of God.

Tashlich appears to be a manifestation of Israel's genius to devise ways of perfecting itself in the service of God.

The Sages say: הַנַּח לָהֶם לְיִשְׂרָאֵל, אִם אֵין נְבִיאִים הֵם בְּנֵי נְבִיאִים הֵם, *Let Israel be, if they are not prophets, they are descendants of prophets* (*Pesachim* 66a). Indeed, the national soul of Israel has its ways of determining how to draw closer to the service of God.

Commentators have advanced reasons for the custom, as we shall see below, but the *primary* reason that *Tashlich* is incumbent upon us is because Israel's usage has ordained the custom's sanctity. As *Rama* (*Toras HaOlah* 3:56) and *Yosef Ometz* (975) say simply: מִנְהַג יִשְׂרָאֵל תּוֹרָה הוּא, *a custom of Israel has the status of Torah.*

The Satanic River

When Abraham was challenged, Satan had carte blanche to impede Abraham by weakening his devotion to God.

BOTH *SHELAH HAKADOSH* (*ROSH HASHANAH, AMUD HaDin*) and *Levush* (*Orach Chaim* 596) cite the same reason for the custom: When Abraham was challenged with the climactic test of his life, God's command to sacrifice Isaac, part of the test was that Satan had *carte blanche* to impede Abraham by weakening his devotion to God. Satan played on the emotions of the aged father who was on the way to give up his beloved heir. Abraham would not be swayed. Finally, Satan placed an impassable river in front of Abraham and Isaac. They forged ahead and went deeper and deeper into the water until it was up to their necks. Abraham was ready to go on — neither logic, water, nor threat of death could deter his resolve, but how could he do God's will if a river were to drown him? He appealed to God, and the river disappeared.

Abraham's determination had defeated Satan, and he continued unhindered to the summit of devotion to God. The *Tashlich* ritual is intended to recall that climactic episode on the way to the *Akeidah*. We go to a river, or some other body of water, to recall before God, and to ourselves, that our forefather defeated the master of evil at a river. Let it remind us of the goal for which we were created, the goal of serving God no matter how potent the force that attempts to dissuade us or force us to do otherwise, no matter how "impossible" it is to do the right thing, because even the most formidable obstacle is but a test of our devotion. And let it remind God that the spiritual seeds of Abraham are implanted within his children. The merit of the *Akeidah*, therefore, is not a reminder of an ancient, irrelevant event, but an indication of an always present reality of Israel's potential for greatness (see *Overview* to *Vayeira, ArtScroll Bereishis II*).

We go to a river, to recall before God, and to ourselves, that our forefather defeated the master of evil at a river.

There is a special symbolism in the fact that Satan resorted to a "river" as his last attempt to force Abraham back. Satan combated Abraham's devotion with the most powerful means at his disposal. According to the *Zohar*, a deep river symbolizes בִּינָה, *understanding*, the ability to plumb the depths of knowledge — to expand, develop, and draw conclusions. "There are waters," the *Zohar* teaches, "that raise wise people, and there are waters that raise fools." Understanding is a precious gift of God, but we know all too well how it can be misused and corrupted to give legitimacy and popularity to foolishness and worse. The key to Abraham's greatness was his understanding of truth; destroy that, and he could be pulled down from his spiritual height.

According to the Zohar, a deep river symbolizes בִּינָה, understanding, the ability to plumb the depths of knowledge.

Crisis of Understanding

HOW DOES ONE FIGHT AN ABRAHAM? AND WHAT WAS the purpose of the battle? As the Midrashim teach, the *Akeidah* was designed to bring into reality an intensified dimension of Abraham's fear of, and devotion to, God. God *knew* what Abraham would do, but human beings are created to act, and, therefore, Abraham had to translate his loyalty into the language of deed in order to reach a higher pinnacle of his greatness. Satan sought to challenge his will, his obedience, his faith. Were Abraham to be prevented from reaching Mount Moriah by wild horses, tidal waves, and stone walls, Satan would not have made his point. He would have made it physically impossible for a human being to fulfill God's will, but he would not have proven the person's unwillingness to sacrifice everything for the sake of God.

Abraham had to translate his loyalty into the language of deed in order to reach a higher pinnacle of his greatness.

In this perspective, we must understand the Satanic river impeding Abraham's progress. Ultimately, the river symbolized the deepest level of understanding, the inexorable intelligence that cried out against every step that Abraham took, saying: "Isaac is your only heir! You waited a lifetime for him! God delivered him to you and Sarah by means of miracles. God promised you posterity through him. How can you, who preached against human sacrifice, slaughter your own son? How can an old father kill his only son

Ultimately, the river symbolized the deepest level of understanding, the inexorable intelligence that cried out against every step that Abraham took.

with his own hands? How can you obey — *even believe in* — the God Who demands this of you?"

These questions constitute a "river" more torrential than any on earth. We can more easily picture Abraham walking across the Amazon at its deepest than we can perceive him negotiating this river of understanding that defied his every attempt to comprehend God's purpose.

Abraham responded with an even higher level of understanding than Satan's. He called out to God for help, "The waters of understanding are up to my neck. They threaten to drown my limited human intelligence. Nevertheless, I know that רֵאשִׁית חָכְמָה יִרְאַת ה', *the beginning of wisdom is fear of* HASHEM (*Psalms* 112:10); the source of wisdom is not what my mortal mind conceives, nor the overwhelmingly compelling logic of Satan. I cannot refute his arguments nor cross his river, because my humanity limits me. But *You,* HASHEM — *You* are my Guide, and when all else fails me, I negate my wisdom to Your will."

By plunging into the river that produced fools, Abraham transformed the event into a river that produced within him — and his offspring — a heightened perception of Israel's mission.

The river disappeared. By plunging into the river that produced fools, Abraham transformed the event into a river that produced within him — and his offspring — a heightened perception of Israel's mission, for to experience truth is far more fulfilling than to philosophize about it.

There is an understanding more compelling than Satan's, an understanding that transcends the narrow limits of human intelligence.

To remember this lesson, *Shelah* and *Levush* teach, the Jewish nation repairs to its rivers and waterways during the most solemn and awesome period of the year. Exactly when and where the first Jews went to the first *Tashlich* we do not know, but it was almost certainly during the Middle Ages when pogrom, inquisition, death, torture, and expulsion were the daily lot of the Jew. One can easily imagine Satan throwing a river of tears and blood in the path of our ancestors and asking questions hardly less difficult than those he asked Abraham. Jews responded as they always have. There is an understanding more compelling than Satan's, an understanding that transcends the narrow limits of human intelligence. "Help us, HASHEM, as You helped Abraham, from the

waters that threaten to inundate our faith, because, like our father, we place our faith in You above all else."

The Coronation

It is a throwback to the ancient custom of Scriptural times when it was customary to crown new kings at riverbanks.

IN THIS PERSPECTIVE, WE CAN BETTER UNDERSTAND ANother reason given for the *Tashlich* custom. *Siddur Otzar HaTefillos* submits that it is a throwback to the ancient custom of Scriptural times when it was customary to crown new kings at riverbanks. Rosh Hashanah is the day when God stands revealed as the *King* Who judges His universe and holds its destiny in His hand. Prayers begin to incorporate this concept on Rosh Hashanah when we describe Him as הַמֶּלֶךְ הַקָּדוֹשׁ, *the Holy King*. The Mussaf *Shemoneh Esrei* includes ten Scriptural verses attesting to His Kingship. *R' Saadiah Gaon* comments that one reason for the *shofar* blast is to approximate the trumpeting tribute to a monarch. Therefore, declares *Otzar HaTefillos,* we trek to a river to crown God, as it were, in the ancient manner of servants accepting upon themselves the sovereignty of their ruler. The *Ten Sefiros* [Emanations] conclude with מַלְכוּת, *Kingship,* the manifestation on earth of God's total mastery of creation. Abraham's tenth trial, the *Akeidah,* was simultaneously the culminating demonstration of his greatness and of God's revelation in human events (see *Overviews* to *Lech Lecha* and *Vayeira, ArtScroll Bereishis II;* and to *Ruth*). Abraham's conquest of the river of misunderstanding was a key element of this manifestation of God's majesty; therefore, it is commemorated by *Tashlich* on the very day God is acknowledged as King.

We trek to a river to crown God, as it were.

Abraham's conquest of the river of misunderstanding was a key element of this manifestation of God's majesty.

II. Eternal Akeidah*

ר׳ חֲנִינָה בֶּן דוֹסָא אוֹמֵר: אוֹתוֹ הָאַיִל לֹא יָצָא מִמֶּנּוּ דָּבָר לְבַטָּלָה. אַפְרוֹ שֶׁל אַיִל הוּא יְסוֹד שֶׁעַל גַּבֵּי מִזְבֵּחַ הַפְּנִימִי... גִידָיו שֶׁל אַיִל הֵם עֲשָׂרָה נִימִין שֶׁל כִּנּוֹר שֶׁהָיָה דָוִד מְנַגֵּן בָּהֶם... עוֹרוֹ שֶׁל אַיִל הוּא אֵזוֹר מָתְנָיו שֶׁל אֵלִיָּהוּ ... שְׁתֵּי קַרְנָיו שֶׁל אַיִל, שֶׁל שְׂמֹאל נִשְׁמַע קוֹלוֹ עַל הַר סִינַי וְקֶרֶן שֶׁל יָמִין הוּא גָדוֹל מִן הַשְּׂמֹאל, וְעָתִיד לִתְקוֹעַ בּוֹ לֶעָתִיד לָבֹא בְּקִבּוּץ שֶׁל גָלֻיּוֹת.

R' Chaninah ben Dosa says: No part of that ram [which Abraham used as a sacrifice at the Akeidah in place of Isaac] went unused. The ashes of the ram were in the top of the inner altar ... the veins of the ram were ten, corresponding to the ten strings of the harp upon which David played... The skin of the ram was the leather belt girdling Elijah's loins ... As for the two horns of the ram, the sound of the left one was heard [as the shofar sound] on Mount Sinai, and the right horn is greater than the left one, and it will be blown in the time to Come when all exiles are gathered together (*Pirkei D'Rabbi Eliezer* Ch. 31).

A Compensatory Deed

Let us attempt to conceive of all the Jewish spiritual accomplishments of the nearly thirty-seven centuries since the Akeidah.

ABRAHAM'S PRIMARY TEST AT THE *AKEIDAH* WAS THE realization that he was to forfeit God's promise that Israel would descend from him. Were the childless Isaac to die, Abraham's life-dream would forever go unrealized. Let us attempt to conceive of all the Jewish spiritual accomplishments of the nearly thirty-seven centuries since the *Akeidah*. Surely an impossible task! All the Torah, all the mitzvos, all the holiness, all the kindness! Thirty-seven centuries worth of achievement by all the hundreds of millions of Jews who have lived since the *Akeidah!*

* [This section of the *Overview* is based on a *shiur* given by Harav Gedaliah Schorr זצ״ל.]

Abraham was ready to substitute one stroke of the knife for all that.

Abraham was ready to substitute one stroke of the knife for all that, if such were God's wish.

Let us view Abraham's potential deed from another perspective. We know that in the world of the spirit, the *quality* of a single mitzvah can often outweigh many, many others. As Abraham advanced upon Mount Moriah, he recognized that the one deed he was preparing to perform would have to be of sufficient quality and of such significance that it would be the equivalent of all the centuries of Jewish life that would never be. There could be no other *spiritual* explanation of the slaughter of the one person who was intended to be the forerunner of God's Chosen People.

The realization was alluded to in Abraham's statement to his servants as he took leave of them and went with Isaac to the summit of Mount Moriah:

אֲנִי וְהַנַּעַר נֵלְכָה עַד כֹּה, *I and the youth* [i.e., *Isaac*] *will go* [כֹּה] *yonder* [lit., *thus*]. *Rashi* comments that the word כֹּה alludes to the earlier promise God had given Abraham: כֹּה יִהְיֶה זַרְעֶךָ, *thus* [like the infinite number of the stars] *will your children be* (*Bereishis* 15:6). As Abraham went up the mountain to offer Isaac as a sacrifice, he had in mind the infinite accomplishments expected of his posterity. He perceived that his one act would have to be the spiritual equivalent of the billions upon billions of good deeds that would never be done. The purpose of Israel's existence is to manifest the majesty of God as King — Abraham, by his conquest of Satan and of his own human, intelligent and paternal feelings, would demonstrate that the only determining factor is the will of the King.

He perceived that his one act would have to be the spiritual equivalent of the billions upon billions of good deeds that would never be done.

As the event developed, however, the *Akeidah* was not to replace Jewish history. Instead, it was to be a seminal event in the very creation of that history, because his devotion then created the pattern of self-sacrifice and courage that has characterized Jewry ever since. Not only has it affected Jewish behavior, but it remains a source of merit for every Jew who has within his heart an ember of the *Akeidah* (*Sfas Emes*).

A Seminal Event

WITH THIS PERSPECTIVE WE CAN BETTER COMPREHEND the disposition of every part of Abraham's ram. His deed did not end when he and Isaac descended the mountain leaving the smoldering ashes of the ram behind him on the altar. By investing his act with the intention of compensating for an immense, future history that might never be, he added new dimensions to — perhaps even made possible — those events of the future. This, then, is the deeper meaning of *Pirkei D'Rabbi Eliezer* cited above:

By investing his act with the intention of compensating for an immense, future history that might never be, he added new dimensions to those events of the future.

— The corners of the Inner Altar, upon which the Kohen Gadol would sprinkle blood of atonement on Yom Kippur, contained the spiritual presence of the ultimate sacrifice Abraham was prepared to make — and, therefore, Israel remains more deserving of atonement even when it falls short of the standard it is meant to achieve.

— David's harp, which played the Sweet Singer's eternal songs of devotion, was strung with the devotion represented by Abraham's ram. Great though he was, without an Abraham there could not have been a David of such stature.

— Elijah girded himself with bravery to defy King Ahab and Queen Jezebel, and their false prophets. By his example he was able to induce all Israel to declare, ה' הוּא הָאֱלֹהִים, ה' הוּא הָאֱלֹהִים, *HASHEM — He is God! HASHEM — He is God* (*I Kings* 18:39)! Elijah succeeded in eliciting this recognition from Israel because he clothed himself with Abraham's manifestation of God's Kingship.

Elijah succeeded in eliciting this recognition from Israel because he clothed himself with Abraham's manifestation of God's Kingship.

— God's Presence on Sinai was proclaimed by a powerful, incessant *shofar* blast. Hearing its call, Israel accepted, and dedicated itself to, the Torah. That resolve, too, was a legacy of Abraham. The *shofar* sound of Sinai alluded to the left and lesser horn of Abraham's ram. The day at Sinai was the lesser of the two greatest days in history, because Israel was not yet fully ready to play the role assigned it. But that day will come . . .

The shofar sound of Sinai alluded to the left and lesser horn of Abraham's ram.

— The *shofar* of Mashiach will be the right horn of Abraham's ram. That will be the שׁוֹפָר גָּדוֹל, *great shofar,*

The right horn will summon even the forlorn and assimilated exiles from earth's most forsaken lands.

that will summon even the forlorn and assimilated exiles from earth's most forsaken lands. Then they will come to Jerusalem, to the mountain of God, to Mount Moriah where Abraham stood at the *Akeidah* and sanctified the present and future for all time.

This is a further manifestation of the principle of מַעֲשֵׂי אָבוֹת סִימָן לַבָּנִים, *the deeds of the Patriarchs are portents for the children* (see *Overview* to *Lech Lecha, ArtScroll Bereishis II*). The lives of their posterity indeed reflect the experiences of the Patriarchs, but to view this phenomenon as an instance of history repeating itself is so superficial as to miss the point entirely. When a seed develops into a plant, history has not merely repeated itself; the seed has *produced* the plant. A bushel of kernels produces a field of grain. Abraham's deeds were the seeds that grew into service at an altar, songs on a harp, courage on a mountain, the announcement of mankind's destiny, the call of creation's fulfillment.

When Jews stand in repentance at a riverbank, they are Abraham advancing into an angry river and erasing every question mark seeking to cloud his faith.

When Jews stand in repentance at a riverbank, an ocean beach, a backyard well, and repent with their *Tashlich* prayer, they are Abraham advancing into an angry river and erasing every question mark seeking to cloud his faith.

III. Lesson of the Depths

THE CORE OF THE *TASHLICH* PRAYER IS THE SELECTION of three verses from *Michah* (7:18-20) which ask the Merciful God to cast Israel's sins בִּמְצֻלוֹת יָם, *into the depths of the sea* (see commentary to *Tashlich*). *Rama* in *Toras HaOlah* finds in this expression a primary reason for the *Tashlich* custom.

The seas are by far the greater part of earth. The waters should have inundated the land and made human life impossible. Indeed, storms and tidal waves give us continuous reminders of the ocean's awesome power. At the beginning of creation, water covered everything; there was no dry land at all until God

commanded that the waters congregate to form seas and expose the land.

The purpose of creation was to provide a habitat for man, a setting where he could exercise his Divinely given intelligence.

That God created an overwhelming mass of water, but decreed the emergence of lands, reveals that the purpose of creation was to provide a habitat for man, a setting where he could exercise his Divinely given intelligence and let his soul be master of his body in God's service. Rosh Hashanah inaugurates the days when man is judged by his Maker. How well has he served God? How well has he utilized the earth and its fullness that God placed at his disposal? How well has he achieved the purpose of his existence?

Standing before the watery deep on the Day of Judgment, a Jew is reawakened to his mission on earth. The commentators cite the further symbolism of having fish in the water at which *Tashlich* is recited (see *Shelah; Magen Avraham* 583; *Ketzei HaMateh* to *Mateh Ephraim* 598). The defenseless fish, prey to every net and hook, remind man that he, too, has no guarantee of safety. The unblinking eyes of the fish suggest the eternally vigilant and merciful eye of God. The fish, covered by the waters and safe from the evil eye of jealousy, allude to Israel, which has been granted God's blessing of protection.

So many prods to the conscience, sensitivity, and awareness of the Jew.

So many reminders. So many prods to the conscience, sensitivity, and awareness of the Jew. So much that unites him as a branch with the Abrahamitic seed from which he sprang. How sad that people, as creatures of habit, are so apt to clutch at ritual and neglect its purpose.

His ancestor once confronted a Satanic river, but refused to let his resolve buckle, thereby planting a seed whose fruits we still harvest.

But no matter what has occurred over so many years and in so many lands, the Jew is reminded on Rosh Hashanah, or on whatever other day he goes to *Tashlich,* that his ancestor once confronted a Satanic river, but refused to let his resolve buckle; and by doing so, he planted a seed whose fruits we still harvest.

Rabbi Nosson Scherman

TASHLICH / סדר תשליך

וחנון	רחום	אל	יהוה	יהוה
AND GRACIOUS.	COMPASSIONATE	GOD,	HASHEM,	HASHEM,

[א] מִי אֵל כָּמוֹךָ [ב] נֹשֵׂא עָוֹן [ג] וְעֹבֵר עַל פֶּשַׁע

[1] Who ‹ is a God ‹ like You, «[2] Who pardons ‹ iniquity ‹ [3] and overlooks ‹ transgression ‹

On the afternoon of the first day of Rosh Hashanah [or on the second day when the first day occurs on Shabbos] after Minchah services, it is customary to go to a river or body of running water — preferably containing live fish, or if impossible, even to a running wellspring — to recite *Tashlich.*

As noted in the commentary, the *Tashlich* service consists primarily of the recitation of verses from *Micah* 7:18-20: מִי אֵל כָּמוֹךָ וגו׳, which Kabbalistically correspond to the Thirteen Divine Attributes in *Exodus* 34:6-7: ה׳ ה׳ אֵל רַחוּם וגו׳ and of verses from *Psalms* 118:5-9: מִן הַמֵּצַר וגו׳, which correspond to the Nine Attributes in *Numbers* 14:18: ה׳ אֶרֶךְ אַפַּיִם וגו׳.

One should concentrate on the corresponding Attributes while reciting these verses, but should not articulate them (*Arizal*).

Attribute 1

מִי אֵל כָּמוֹךָ — *Who is a God like You?* The translation follows *Malbim. Targum* paraphrases: There is no one but You, You alone are God. According to this rendering, the prophet directly addresses God and expresses his recognition that He is incomparable.

Others, however, do not designate אֵל as a Divine Name referring to God, but as a non-sacred word meaning *god* or *power. Who is a god like You?* Thus, the prophet tells God that nothing — idol, angel, or natural force — is like Him (*Ibn Ezra; Metzudas David*).

Tomer Devorah explains that the Holy One, Blessed is He, is incomparable in His patience. To a degree beyond human understanding, he endures human behavior that, by its very nature, is insolent and insulting in the extreme. Consider that at every moment of man's existence, he is dependent on the Divine gifts of life and strength. It is man's responsibility to utilize these gifts in the service of God. Thus, when man sins against God, it is God's *own* strength that man turns against his Maker! Although this strength is used for sin, God does not withhold it from man, saying, "If you choose to offend Me, you may not do so with the power I have granted you." God is unlike any other power in the world: He patiently bears insult and sustains life that is used *against* Him — in the hope that man will repent.

Every man should emulate this Attribute by training himself to be patient, to bear insult, and even to bestow kindness upon those who abuse him.

Attribute 2

נֹשֵׂא עָוֹן — *Who pardons* [lit., *bears*] *iniquity.* This Attribute surpasses the preceding quality of patience, for an angel of destruction is created every time a man sins. *Avos* (4:11) teaches: He who commits a wrongdoing acquires a prosecutor for himself; this angel stands accusingly before the Holy One, Blessed is He, and says, "That sinner created me."

Who supplies the vital energy that allows this evil force to exist? God Himself! He could refuse to nourish the destructive angel, by saying, "Go sap the life of the sinner who created you and exist on that." Were this to happen, the sinner would be destroyed by the very nemesis he brought into being. But God is compassionate. He is נֹשֵׂא עָוֹן, literally, He *bears* or *carries iniquity,* [i.e., the destructive angel created by the sin]; He nourishes and sustains the evil force, so that the sinner may continue to live and have the opportunity to repent.

From this, man should learn tolerance. Even when his neighbor offends him and even when the results of the offense are still in existence, the victim of wrongdoing should not harm his neighbor, but rather should wait patiently for the wrong to be righted.

Attribute 3

וְעֹבֵר עַל פֶּשַׁע — *And overlooks* [lit., *passes over*] *transgression* [lit., *rebellion*]. It is God Himself Who grants forgiveness. He does not

ארך — SLOW; אפים — TO ANGER,

[ד] לִשְׁאֵרִית נַחֲלָתוֹ [ה] לֹא הֶחֱזִיק לָעַד אַפּוֹ

[4] for the remnant ‹ of His heritage? « [5] He has not ‹ retained ‹ eternally ‹ His wrath, «

ורב חסד — AND ABUNDANT IN KINDNESS; ואמת — AND TRUTH,

[ו] כִּי חָפֵץ חֶסֶד הוּא. [ז] יָשׁוּב יְרַחֲמֵנוּ

[6] for ‹ desirous ‹ of kindness ‹ is He. « [7] He will again ‹ be merciful to us; «

delegate this important function to a deputy or agent, as Scripture states: כִּי עִמְּךָ הַסְּלִיחָה, *For with You is the forgiveness* (*Psalms* 130:4). Furthermore, God Himself pours out clean water, as it were, to wash away the stains of sin. How shameful sin is, for the sinner obliges the Holy King *Himself* to cleanse his filthy garments!

This Attribute teaches man to be willing to rectify the damage caused by the sins of other men. Since every crime or perversion is an affront to God, man must strive to correct each offense, even if the act was not his own responsibility. Would we hesitate to save our neighbor's house from fire because we did not set the blaze?

◆§ Attribute 4

לִשְׁאֵרִית נַחֲלָתוֹ — *For the remnant of His heritage.* The word שְׁאֵר means both *remnant* and *blood relative.* The prophet directs his words to the *remnant* of Israel who survived the long exile and who will receive special Divine kindness (*Radak*).

God loves Israel as if the Jewish nation were a close relative. He calls her, "My daughter," "My sister," and "My mother." Thus, the psalmist describes the Jews as בְּנֵי יִשְׂרָאֵל עַם קְרֹבוֹ, *The Children of Israel: the nation related to Him* (*Psalms* 148:14).

God says, "How can I punish Israel when her pain will be Mine?" The prophet states: *In all their sorrows He is afflicted* (*Isaiah* 63:9). God cannot bear Israel's pain or disgrace for it is His *remnant*, all that He has in His universe. From God's love for us, a Jew learns how to love his fellow man. All Jews are related to each other; their souls are united, and in each soul there is a portion of all the others. For this reason, all Jews are responsible for one another (*Shevuos* 39a). Since each Jewish soul possesses a portion of all the others, when an Israelite sins, his wrong affects not only *his own* soul, but also the portion that all the others possess in him. It follows, therefore, that every Jew should love his neighbor as he loves himself, for he and his neighbor are one.

◆§ Attribute 5

לֹא הֶחֱזִיק לָעַד אַפּוֹ — *He has not retained eternally His wrath.* The שְׁאָר, *remnant*, who endured the exile, are unworthy of redemption because they continue to be guilty of many of the shortcomings for which their fathers were first exiled. Nevertheless, God does not retain His wrath against them eternally (*Radak*).

This is another unique form of Divine mercy. Even when a man persists in sinning, God does not persist in retaining His anger. He allows His anger to abate even when man does not repent.

Man should employ this Attribute when dealing with his neighbors. Even when he has the right to rebuke his neighbor, he should not persist in his rebuke nor continue his anger; he should end his wrath as soon as possible.

◆§ Attribute 6

כִּי חָפֵץ חֶסֶד הוּא — *For desirous of kindness is He.* The Torah states, וְרַב חֶסֶד, *And He is abundant in kindness* (*Exodus* 34:6). When the time arrives for the redemption of Israel, God's kindness will overwhelm their sins (*Radak*).

Tomer Devorah comments that God has appointed special angels whose task is to gather in all the acts of kindness that Israel performs and to place them in a celestial treasury, as it were. When Israel's misconduct earns the accusations of the Attribute of Strict Justice,

נצר חסד
FOR THOUSANDS [OF GENERATIONS]

לאלפים
PRESERVER OF KINDNESS

[ח] יִכְבֹּשׁ עֲוֹנֹתֵינוּ [ט] וְתַשְׁלִיךְ בִּמְצֻלוֹת יָם כָּל חַטֹּאתָם.

[8] He will suppress 〈 our iniquities. 《 [9] And You will cast 〈 into the depths 〈 of the sea 〈 all 〈 their sins. 《

these angels immediately bring Israel's kindness to the attention of the Almighty.

God delights in the acts of kindness that Jews perform for one another and remembers this aspect of their character even when they are guilty in other respects.

Man should imitate God's kindness. When he is hurt or provoked, let him look at the offender's good and admirable qualities (especially the quality of kindness to others). Then let him say, "It is enough for me that he has shown kindness to another, or that he has some other fine trait." Thus, He will delight in kindness.

☙ Attribute 7

יָשׁוּב יְרַחֲמֵנוּ — *He will again be merciful to us.* Divine behavior differs from that of mortals. When a man has been offended, he cannot bring himself to love the one who offended him as much as he formerly did. But in the eyes of God, the repentant sinner enjoys a higher status than the man who has never sinned. As the Talmud (*Berachos* 34b) teaches: In the place and on the level where the penitent stands, the perfectly righteous cannot stand.

For those who have not sinned, a slight fence is sufficient to act as a barrier against sin. But such a barrier will not suffice for the penitent sinner. He must be very far removed from sin, lest the evil inclination tempt him again. Consequently, he must ascend higher and higher, closer and closer to God, in order to be shielded from further wrongdoing. Thus, יָשׁוּב, *when he* [the penitent] *returns* to God, God's love will increase more and more, and יָשׁוּב יְרַחֲמֵנוּ, *God will return* [and reciprocate] and be even more *merciful to us.* This is a guide for a man's behavior toward his neighbor. If his neighbor offended him but afterward sought reconciliation, he should show him a greater degree of kindness than he did previously. He should encourage this neighbor even more than he would a perfectly righteous acquaintance who had never hurt him.

☙ Attribute 8

יִכְבֹּשׁ עֲוֹנֹתֵינוּ — *He will suppress our iniquities.* When a man fulfills a precept, he creates a powerful, flourishing force that grows until it enters God's celestial Presence. Sins, however, have no entry there, for God subdues and rejects them. The psalmist states: כִּי לֹא אֵל חָפֵץ רֶשַׁע אָתָּה לֹא יְגֻרְךָ רָע, *For You are not a god who desires wickedness, no evil sojourns with You* (*Psalms* 5:5). Thus, there is no reward in This World for performing a mitzvah (*Kiddushin* 39b), because the precept reaches God's heavenly Presence. The entire mundane world is not equal to the spiritual value of a single good deed. Furthermore, no limited earthly reward can compare to the infinite spiritual rewards of the World to Come.

God does not allow sins to cancel the effect of mitzvos. He does not say, "Ten sins negate ten mitzvos," so that the account is closed with neither punishment nor reward. Mitzvos are too precious to be cast aside so offhandedly. How can a sin, a mundane crime, cancel out a good deed that ascends to the highest heavens? God suppresses our iniquities so that they do not rise before Him. Although the sins will be punished in this lower world, the reward for mitzvos is reserved for the world of the spirit.

Similarly, a man should suppress the memory of any evil that was done to him, but remember every kindness. The good deeds should always be uppermost in his mind, so that he may sincerely appreciate them.

☙ Attribute 9

וְתַשְׁלִיךְ בִּמְצֻלוֹת יָם כָּל חַטֹּאתָם — *And You will cast into the depths of the sea all their* sins. It is from these words that the *Tashlich* ritual derives its name. This ninth Attribute, as

(וְכָל חַטֹּאת עַמְּךָ בֵּית יִשְׂרָאֵל, תַּשְׁלִיךְ בִּמְקוֹם

‹ to a place ‹ cast away ‹ of Israel, ‹ the House ‹ of Your people, ‹ the sins ‹ (And all

אֲשֶׁר לֹא יִזָּכְרוּ, וְלֹא יִפָּקְדוּ, וְלֹא יַעֲלוּ עַל לֵב לְעוֹלָם.)

« ever.) ‹ mind ‹ to ‹ be brought ‹ nor ‹ be considered, ‹ nor ‹ be remembered, ‹ they will not ‹ where

ופשע
WILLFUL SIN

נשא עון
FORGIVER OF INIQUITY,

[י] תִּתֵּן אֱמֶת לְיַעֲקֹב [יא] חֶסֶד לְאַבְרָהָם [יב] אֲשֶׁר

‹ **as [12]** « **to Abraham,** ‹ **kindness [11]** « **to Jacob,** ‹ **truth** ‹ **Grant [10]**

described by *Tomer Devorah,* demonstrates how man may actually shed his sins and cast them away.

Good men and evil deeds are an incongruous mixture. A Jew is innately good; his essence does not become evil despite his having sinned. Therefore, when a good man repents and purges himself of evil, the evil departs from him and returns to the spiritual depths, the realm of evil.

This is the secret of the Yom Kippur offering, of which it is written: *And the goat shall bear upon himself all of their iniquities and take them to a barren land* (*Leviticus* 16:22).

The goat represents the forces of evil. Evil belongs to the forces of evil — to the barren wilderness — and not to Israel. When Israel sins, it, in effect, takes something — evil — that does not belong to it. When Israel repents, it sends the evil back to the source of evil, as if it is repaying a debt.

The wicked are likened to the raging sea, as the prophet said: *The wicked are like the troubled sea, for it cannot rest; its waters cast up mire and dirt* (*Isaiah* 57:20). Thus, the prophet Micah says, in effect, "You will cast all of Israel's sins upon the wicked, who are likened to the muddy depths of the sea."

A man can emulate this Attribute. If he notices that his neighbor is crushed by suffering as a result of his sins, he should not disdain him for it. Rather, he should realize that suffering cleanses a man of sin and causes the evil to depart and to return to its source.

☙ Attribute 10

תִּתֵּן אֱמֶת לְיַעֲקֹב — *Grant truth to Jacob.* Average, ordinary people who do not go beyond the letter of the law are called *Jacob,* for Jacob was a symbol of exact honesty. The name *Israel* is reserved for those who strive for extraordinary excellence.

God, too, possesses a quality of truth that follows the dictates of strict justice. Even for those who conduct themselves with precise truth as defined by the halachah, God exercises compassion, but only in accordance with His rigid standards of truth.

Every man should treat his neighbor with truth, and refuse to pervert justice. Thus even the average man will be perfected in accordance with the quality of truth.

☙ Attribute 11

חֶסֶד לְאַבְרָהָם — *Kindness to Abraham.* This refers to the righteous people who go beyond the letter of the law, as did the Patriarch Abraham. God reciprocates and behaves toward these people with *kindness* beyond the letter of the law.

When dealing with average men, a person should conduct himself with strict justice and truth. But when he comes in contact with those who are outstanding in their devotion to God, he should exceed the requirements of the law. If he is only slightly patient with ordinary men, he should strive to be exceptionally patient with the exceptionally devout. Such unique people should be exceedingly beloved to him.

☙ Attribute 12

אֲשֶׁר נִשְׁבַּעְתָּ לַאֲבֹתֵינוּ — *As You swore to our forefathers.* The Holy One, Blessed is He, has mercy even upon the undeserving, because God swore to their forefathers that He would

ונקה AND WHO ABSOLVES — וחטאה AND INADVERTENT SIN,

נִשְׁבַּעְתָּ לַאֲבֹתֵינוּ [יג] **מִימֵי קֶדֶם.**[1]

« of old. ‹ from days [13] ‹ to our forefathers ‹ You swore

אפים TO ANGER, — יהוה ארך HASHEM, SLOW

[א] **מִן הַמֵּצַר קָרָאתִי יָּהּ*** [ב] **עָנָנִי בַמֶּרְחָב יָהּ.***

[1] In distress* › I called upon › God; » [2] answered me › with abounding relief › did God.* »

(1) *Micah* 7:18-20.

care for their descendants. In heaven, God has a special storehouse of grace, as it were, reserved for those who are unworthy; they receive this grace as an unearned gift.

Similarly, when a man meets an evildoer, he should not spurn him. Rather he should be gracious, saying, "No matter what this man does, he remains the son of Abraham, Isaac, and Jacob. Even if he is unworthy, his forefathers were worthy. He who brings disgrace upon the children brings disgrace upon the fathers, and I have no desire to have the holy Patriarchs humiliated through me."

Attribute 13

מִימֵי קֶדֶם — *From days of old.* If the merit of the forefathers is ever exhausted [see *Shabbos* 55a and *Tosafos,* s.v. וּשְׁמוּאֵל] and Israel is unworthy, what will God do? Israel has its *own* merit. It is written: ,זָכַרְתִּי לָךְ חֶסֶד נְעוּרַיִךְ אַהֲבַת כְּלוּלֹתָיִךְ, לֶכְתֵּךְ אַחֲרַי בַּמִּדְבָּר, *I remember in your favor the kindness of your youth, your love as a bride when you followed after Me into the wilderness (Jeremiah* 2:2). God recalls all the good deeds that Israel performed from the day of its inception and He will relate to it with all His merciful Attributes.

A man should conduct himself in similar fashion when he encounters a person who seems to be totally devoid of any redeeming virtue. He should say, "Surely there was a time when this man had not yet sinned. Surely, in his early youth, while he was still uncorrupted, he performed some good deeds." Using this Attribute, no man will be found unworthy of goodness and mercy.

These are the Thirteen Attributes by which man can imitate the Creator. If man emulates these Attributes on earth, he will trigger the higher Attribute of Mercy from above, and cause the Divine quality of mercy to shine upon the world. Therefore, repeat and remember these Attributes, exhorts *Tomer Devorah,* so that they may be a constant reminder to follow in God's ways.

According to Kabbalah, Moses invoked nine Attributes when he pleaded with God not to destroy Israel for its acceptance of the evil report of the מְרַגְּלִים, *spies.* These correspond to the nine Attributes that the Kabbalists perceived in the selection from Psalms that follows. Again, the accounting of the Attributes follows the opinion of the *Arizal,* and the Attributes derived from the Torah are written above those from the *Psalms.*

Attribute 1

מִן הַמֵּצַר קָרָאתִי יָּהּ — *In distress I called upon God.* This selection from *Psalms* reflects the theme of Rosh Hashanah. Its first verse is also recited to introduce the blowing of the *shofar.* As the threat of harsh Divine judgment looms over the Jewish people on Rosh Hashanah, they are indeed in deep distress. But when they sense that sincere repentance has removed their heavy burden of sin, they know that God has answered them.

This concept corresponds to the symbolic casting away of sin, which is the theme of *Tashlich.*

Radak attributes these words to David, who was hiding in narrow and distressing caves [מֵצַר from צַר, *constriction*] during his flight from Saul.

During that time of woe and *distress,* God did not reveal His full Presence to David.

ופשע	נשא עון	ורב חסד
WILLFUL SIN,	FORGIVER OF INIQUITY,	AND ABUNDANT IN KINDNESS

[ג] יהוה לִי [ד] לֹא אִירָא* [ה] מַה יַּעֲשֶׂה לִי אָדָם.*

[3] HASHEM ‹ is with me, ‹ [4] I have no fear;* « [5] how ‹ can man affect me?* «

לא ינקה	ונקה
BUT DOES NOT ABSOLVE [COMPLETELY]	AND WHO ABSOLVES

[ו] יהוה לִי בְּעֹזְרָי* [ז] וַאֲנִי אֶרְאֶה בְשֹׂנְאָי.*

[6] HASHEM ‹ is with me ‹ through my helpers;* « [7] therefore I ‹ can face ‹ my foes.* «

Therefore, David did not refer to God with His full Name, Hashem, but with the partial Divine Name יָהּ, *Yah*. Eventually, *Yah* did answer David *with abounding relief*, despite the fact that the Divine Presence was in eclipse (*Alshich*).

Radak suggests that the verse can also be understood as the collective plea of the Jews in exile. *Abarbanel* adds that the Jews here recall the difficult days in the מֵצַר of מִצְרַיִם, *Egypt*. [מִצְרַיִם may be read as מְצָרִים, *limits; straits.*] Just as God responded at that time when we called out to Him, so does He respond whenever we plead before Him in distress.

Attribute 2

עָנָנִי בַמֶּרְחָב יָהּ — *Answered me with abounding relief did God.* [In *Psalms* 4:2 we read: בַּצָּר הִרְחַבְתָּ לִּי, *You have relieved me of my distress.* צַר, *distress,* literally means *a tight, constricted place,* and הִרְחַבְתָּ, *relieved,* literally means *widened, enlarged.*

David said to the Holy One, Blessed is He, "Master of the universe, whenever I was constricted by difficult circumstances, You provided an avenue of relief and set me free. When I was caught in the dilemma of Bat-sheva, You presented me with a wonderful son, Solomon. When I was embroiled in the distress of all Israel, You eased my burden and gave me permission to prepare for the construction of the Holy Temple" (*Yerushalmi Taanis* 2:9).

This declaration is an eloquent expression of one of David's most cherished credos: Never be discouraged by the terrible burdens and pressures of life, for every frustrating, enfeebling situation is actually a Divinely ordained opportunity to overcome adversity by fully utilizing one's talents and abilities. Thus, every distress that threatens to limit or diminish an individual can serve to broaden his scope and to enlarge his soul. (See commentary to ArtScroll *Tehillim, Psalms* 4:2.)

Attributes 3-4

יהוה לִי — *Hashem is with me.*

לֹא אִירָא — *I have no fear.* God answered me [in the past] with abounding relief despite the fact that His Name was incomplete and His power was partially hidden. Therefore, when the full Name of Hashem is *with me, I [certainly] have no fear* (*Alshich*).

Attribute 5

מַה יַּעֲשֶׂה לִי אָדָם — *What can man do to me?* [Alternatively: *How can man affect* me?]

No individual can harm me *(Radak)*. Even an entire nation cannot overwhelm me or tear me from my faith (*Sforno*).

[Man derives all his strength from God. If God has not ordained my death, how can my adversary destroy me?]

Abraham asked, "What can my enemy Abimelech do to me?"

Jacob asked, "What can my malicious brother Esau do to me?"

David asked, "What can my gigantic rival Goliath do to me?"

This may be compared to the king's favored attendant who was envied by the other courtiers. When they grew jealous and threatened his life, the favorite merely said, "The king loves me and protects me. What, then, can the others do to me?" *(Midrash Shocher Tov)*.

Attribute 6

יהוה לִי בְּעֹזְרָי — *Hashem is with me, through my helpers* [lit., *Hashem* is *with me, among my helpers*]. I have many helpers, but I place

פקד עון אבות על בנים

RECALLING THE INIQUITY OF THE FATHERS ON THE SONS

[ח] **טוֹב לַחֲסוֹת בַּיהוה, מִבְּטֹחַ בָּאָדָם.***

[8] It is better 〈 to take refuge 〈 in Hashem 《 than to rely 〈 on man.* 《

על שלשים ועל רבעים

TO THE THIRD AND TO THE FOURTH [GENERATIONS].

[ט] **טוֹב לַחֲסוֹת בַּיהוה, מִבְּטֹחַ בִּנְדִיבִים.*[1]**

[9] It is better 〈 to take refuge 〈 in Hashem 《 than to rely 〈 on nobles.* 《

(1) *Psalms* 118:5-9.

confidence in them *only* because Hashem is with them. If my helpers were not granted strength by God, their assistance would be futile and worthless *(Ibn Ezra)*.

R' Vidal HaTzorfati and *Chasam Sofer* explain that although man can protect himself from his known enemies (*I shall see the downfall of my enemies*), he is still vulnerable to attack by those adversaries who pose as friends.

Therefore the psalmist asks ,ה׳ לִי, Hashem *be for me*, בְּעֹזְרָי, *for my* [ostensible] *helpers*, i.e., save me from false and treacherous friends.

Attribute 7

וַאֲנִי אֶרְאֶה בְשֹׂנְאָי — *So I shall see* [*the downfall of*] *my enemies*. [Alternatively: *Therefore I can face my foes*.]

Radak notes that the psalmist says something similar in *Psalms* 54:9: *From every distress He has rescued me, and upon my foes my eye has looked.*

The Sages teach that a person who *deserves* salvation is granted the privilege of witnessing the downfall of his enemies, as when Israel saw the death of the Egyptians at the Sea. However, he who is saved by the merits of others does not deserve this privilege. Therefore, Lot, who was saved by virtue of Abraham's merit, was forbidden to look back upon the destruction of Sodom. Here the psalmist expresses confidence that he will be righteous enough to witness his enemies' defeat (*Navah Tehillah*).

R' Yoseif Leib Bloch of Telshe interprets the verse homiletically: It is a common maxim that a person is known through his enemies. If his enemies are righteous people, then he must be at fault, but if he is hated by the wicked, then he must be virtuous. The psalmist expresses his confidence that God will be among his helpers because *I see my enemies*, i.e., since my enemies are the wicked who defy God, I am sure that I am virtuous and worthy of His help. [See *The Haggadah Treasury*.]

Attribute 8

טוֹב לַחֲסוֹת בַּיהוה, מִבְּטֹחַ בָּאָדָם — *It is better to take refuge in Hashem than to rely on man. Rabbeinu Bachya* and *Vilna Gaon*, explain the difference between the two closely related words חִסָּיוֹן, *taking refuge*, and בִּטָּחוֹן, *reliance*. The former denotes absolute confidence, even though no guarantees have been given. The latter presupposes a promise of protection, such as a pledge given by a powerful military or political figure.

The psalmist says that it is far better to trust in God's protection [even if God has made no explicit commitment] than to rely on the most generous assurance of any mortal.

Radak cites the words of the prophet *Jeremiah* (17:5): *Cursed be the person who relies on man and makes mortal flesh his supporting arm.* Even if circumstances do force a person to rely on his fellow man, he should place his main confidence in God, for it is He Who implants the desire to help in the heart of the human benefactor.

Attribute 9

טוֹב לַחֲסוֹת בַּיהוה, מִבְּטֹחַ בִּנְדִיבִים — *It is better to take refuge in Hashem than to rely on nobles. Ibn Ezra* identifies the נְדִיבִים as the dignitaries whose prestige surpasses that of

Psalm 33 / תהלים לג

רַנְּנוּ צַדִּיקִים* בַּיהוה, לַיְשָׁרִים נָאוָה תְהִלָּה. הוֹדוּ

‹ Give thanks « is praise. ‹ fitting ‹ for the upright, « because of HASHEM; ‹ O righteous,* ‹ Sing joyfully,

לַיהוה בְּכִנּוֹר, בְּנֵבֶל עָשׂוֹר זַמְּרוּ לוֹ. שִׁירוּ לוֹ שִׁיר

‹ a song ‹ Him ‹ Sing « to Him. ‹ make music ‹ with a ten-stringed lyre « with a harp, ‹ to HASHEM

חָדָשׁ, הֵיטִיבוּ נַגֵּן בִּתְרוּעָה. כִּי יָשָׁר דְּבַר יהוה,

‹ of HASHEM, ‹ is the word ‹ upright ‹ For « with sounds of deep emotion. ‹ play well « that is new,

וְכָל מַעֲשֵׂהוּ בֶּאֱמוּנָה.* אֹהֵב צְדָקָה וּמִשְׁפָּט, חֶסֶד

‹ the kindness « and justice; ‹ righteousness ‹ He loves « [are done] with faithfulness.* ‹ His deeds ‹ and all

יהוה מָלְאָה הָאָרֶץ. בִּדְבַר יהוה שָׁמַיִם נַעֲשׂוּ,

« were made, ‹ the heavens ‹ of HASHEM ‹ By the word « the earth. ‹ fills ‹ of HASHEM

וּבְרוּחַ פִּיו כָּל צְבָאָם. כֹּנֵס כַּנֵּד מֵי הַיָּם, נֹתֵן

‹ He places « of the sea, ‹ the waters ‹ like a mound ‹ He assembles « their host. ‹ all ‹ of His mouth ‹ and by the breath

בְּאוֹצָרוֹת תְּהוֹמוֹת. יִירְאוּ מֵיהוה כָּל הָאָרֶץ, מִמֶּנּוּ יָגוּרוּ

‹ be in dread, ‹ of Him « the earth; ‹ all ‹ HASHEM, ‹ Fear « the deep waters. ‹ in vaults

כָּל יֹשְׁבֵי תֵבֵל. כִּי הוּא אָמַר וַיֶּהִי, הוּא צִוָּה וַיַּעֲמֹד.*

« and it endured.* ‹ commanded ‹ He « and it came to be; ‹ spoke ‹ He ‹ For « of the world. ‹ inhabitants ‹ all

יהוה הֵפִיר עֲצַת גּוֹיִם, הֵנִיא מַחְשְׁבוֹת עַמִּים. עֲצַת

‹ The counsel « of peoples. ‹ the designs ‹ He thwarts « of nations; ‹ the counsel ‹ annuls ‹ HASHEM

יהוה לְעוֹלָם תַּעֲמֹד, מַחְשְׁבוֹת לִבּוֹ לְדֹר וָדֹר. אַשְׁרֵי

‹ Praiseworthy « to generation. ‹ from generation ‹ of His heart, ‹ the designs « will endure, ‹ forever ‹ of HASHEM

---

all other men. *Ibn Yachya* determines that the נְדִיבִים are the seventy ministering angels, who are God's agents for governing the seventy peoples of the earth.

These seventy angels compose the Heavenly Tribunal that surrounds God's celestial throne. Those who are positioned on God's left are harsh and unrelenting in their demands for strict justice, whereas those who stand at God's right are נְדִיבִים [lit., *generous*] in their desire to treat mankind with compassion.

Nevertheless, it is far better *to take refuge in the mercy of Hashem than to rely on [the kindness of these] noble angels* (*Mahari Giktalia*).

רַנְּנוּ צַדִּיקִים — *Sing joyfully, O righteous.* We turn now to the celebration of the World

הַגּוֹי אֲשֶׁר יהוה אֱלֹהָיו, הָעָם בָּחַר לְנַחֲלָה לוֹ. מִשָּׁמַיִם

‹ From heaven « for Him. ‹ as a heritage. ‹ He chose ‹ the people « is their God, ‹ HASHEM ‹ that ‹ is the nation

הִבִּיט יהוה,* רָאָה אֶת כָּל בְּנֵי הָאָדָם. מִמְּכוֹן שִׁבְתּוֹ

‹ of dwelling ‹ From His place « mankind. ‹ all ‹ He sees « HASHEM looks down,*

הִשְׁגִּיחַ,* אֶל כָּל יֹשְׁבֵי הָאָרֶץ. הַיֹּצֵר יַחַד לִבָּם,

« their hearts, ‹ together ‹ He Who fashions « of the earth. ‹ inhabitants ‹ all ‹ He oversees*

הַמֵּבִין אֶל כָּל מַעֲשֵׂיהֶם. אֵין הַמֶּלֶךְ נוֹשָׁע בְּרָב חָיִל,

« army; ‹ by a great ‹ saved ‹ A king is not « their deeds. ‹ all ‹ Who comprehends

גִּבּוֹר לֹא יִנָּצֵל בְּרָב כֹּחַ. שֶׁקֶר הַסּוּס לִתְשׁוּעָה,

« for salvation; ‹ is the horse ‹ Illusory « strength. ‹ by great ‹ rescued ‹ is not ‹ a hero

וּבְרֹב חֵילוֹ לֹא יְמַלֵּט. הִנֵּה עֵין יהוה אֶל יְרֵאָיו,

« those who fear Him, ‹ is on ‹ of HASHEM ‹ the eye ‹ Indeed, « escape. ‹ no ‹ strength [it provides] ‹ despite its great

לַמְיַחֲלִים לְחַסְדּוֹ. לְהַצִּיל מִמָּוֶת נַפְשָׁם, וּלְחַיּוֹתָם בָּרָעָב.

« in famine. ‹ and to sustain them « their soul, ‹ from death ‹ To rescue « His kindness. ‹ upon those who await

נַפְשֵׁנוּ חִכְּתָה לַיהוה, עֶזְרֵנוּ וּמָגִנֵּנוּ הוּא. כִּי בוֹ

‹ in Him ‹ For « is He. ‹ and our shield ‹ our help « for HASHEM; ‹ longed ‹ Our soul

יִשְׂמַח לִבֵּנוּ, כִּי בְשֵׁם קָדְשׁוֹ בָטָחְנוּ. יְהִי חַסְדְּךָ

‹ Your kindness, ‹ May « we trusted. ‹ in His Holy Name ‹ for « our hearts; ‹ will be gladdened

יהוה עָלֵינוּ, כַּאֲשֶׁר יִחַלְנוּ לָךְ.

« You. ‹ we awaited ‹ just as « be upon us, ‹ HASHEM,

---

to Come when all will recognize that God controls events.

וְכָל מַעֲשֵׂהוּ בֶּאֱמוּנָה — *And all His deeds [are done] with faithfulness.* The natural forces are reliable and consistent. Otherwise we would be in constant fear of upheaval (*Malbim*).

הוּא צִוָּה וַיַּעֲמֹד — *He commanded and it endured* (lit., *stood*). When God ordered the world to come into being, it kept expanding until it reached the size He desired; then He commanded it to stand firm (*Chagigah* 12a).

הִבִּיט ה׳ ... הִשְׁגִּיחַ — *HASHEM looks down ... He oversees.* These expressions imply the two differing forms of God's הַשְׁגָּחָה, *supervision.* There is the general supervision [הַשְׁגָּחָה כְּלָלִית] of the laws of nature; in that sense, God seems to *look down* from a distance. But God also exercises close supervision [הַשְׁגָּחָה פְּרָטִית] — *He oversees* — over each person according to his own deeds (*Malbim*).

THE FOLLOWING SUPPLICATIONS WERE ADDED TO *TASHLICH* BY *CHIDA*. SOME OMIT THEM AND CONCLUDE *TASHLICH* WITH לֹא יָרֵעוּ, ON PAGE 27.

רִבּוֹנוֹ שֶׁל עוֹלָם,* בְּהַעֲלוֹתֵנוּ עַל לְבָבֵנוּ רֹב קְצוֹרֵנוּ

Master ‹ of the ‹ universe,* « when we bring ‹ to ‹ mind ‹ our abundant deficiency ‹

בַּעֲבוֹדָתֶךָ וּבְעֵסֶק תּוֹרָתְךָ הַקְּדוֹשָׁה וְקִיּוּם מִצְוֹתֶיךָ,*

in Your service, « in [our] involvement ‹ with Your Torah ‹ that is holy, « and in [our] fulfillment ‹ of Your commandments,* «

כָּל עַצְמוֹתֵינוּ יֹאחֲזֵמוֹ רָעַד וְנָמֵס לִבֵּנוּ וְהָיָה לַמָּיִם.[1]

all ‹ of our bones ‹ are gripped ‹ with trembling, « and melt ‹ does our heart ‹ and it becomes ‹ like water. «

מַה נַּעֲנֶה וּמַה נֹּאמַר, כִּי הַצָּר הַצּוֹרֵר* בְּחֶבְרַת

What ‹ can we answer? « What ‹ can we say? « For ‹ it is the Adversary ‹ who is the tormentor,* « accompanied by ‹

הַחֹמֶר הֶעָכוּר הָיָה בְּעָכְרֵנוּ,* גַּם אָסוּר נִלְוָה עִמָּם*[2]

our sordid materialism ‹ that caused ‹ our defilement.* « Also ‹ forbidden things ‹ joined ‹ with them* «

אֲסוּרִים וּלְטוּשִׁים*[3] בְּגָלֻיּוֹת קָשִׁים, גָּלוּת הַנֶּפֶשׁ וְהַגּוּף.

— forbidden ‹ and burnished* ‹ in exiles ‹ that are harsh — « [causing] estrangement ‹ of soul ‹ and body. «

---

(1) Cf. *Joshua* 7:5. (2) Cf. *Psalms* 83:9. (3) Cf. *Genesis* 25:3.

⊰ רִבּוֹנוֹ שֶׁל עוֹלָם / Master of the universe.

In the following section, the supplicant bemoans the frailty of man who is beset by a host of powerful lusts and overwhelming desires. *Mesillas Yesharim* (Chapter 1) describes the incessant struggle confronting man:

God placed man in the midst of a raging battle, because all of the affairs of this world, whether for good or evil, are trials to a man. Every life circumstance — wealth or poverty, serenity or suffering — contains its own challenge. The fierce battle rages against man to the fore and to the rear. If he is valorous and victorious on all sides, he will emerge as the אָדָם הַשָּׁלֵם, *the complete man.*

Chovos HaLevavos (*Shaar Yichud HaMa'aseh* 5) tells of the pious man who went out to greet the troops returning from the battlefront. He said to them, "You are returning from a minor skirmish to enter into the major battle — man's lifelong struggle against his evil inclination."

בְּהַעֲלוֹתֵנוּ עַל לְבָבֵנוּ רוֹב קְצוֹרֵנוּ בַּעֲבוֹדָתֶךָ, וּבְעֵסֶק תּוֹרָתְךָ הַקְּדוֹשָׁה, וְקִיּוּם מִצְוֹתֶיךָ — *When we bring to mind our abundant deficiency in Your service, in [our] involvement with Your Torah that is holy, and in [our] fulfillment of Your commandments.* Our debt to God is limitless, but we are woefully limited. How can we ever fully discharge our obligations to Him?

כִּי הַצָּר הַצּוֹרֵר — *It is the Adversary who is the tormentor.* The evil inclination is man's most powerful tormentor and adversary. The Talmud (*Kiddushin* 30b) observes that even God — Creator of the evil inclination — calls it *evil.* This desire renews its assault every day, attempting to overwhelm man and destroy him. If man did not receive Divine assistance, he could not withstand these incessant attacks.

בְּחֶבְרַת הַחוֹמֶר הֶעָכוּר הָיוּ בְעוֹכְרֵינוּ — *Accompanied by our sordid materialism that caused our defilement!* On describing the trait of נְקִיּוּת, *cleanliness, Mesillas Yesharim* (Ch.

הַאֻמְנָם גָּלוּי וְיָדוּעַ לְפָנֶיךָ שֶׁרְצוֹנֵנוּ לַעֲשׂוֹת רְצוֹנֶךָ*[1]

« However, ‹ it is revealed ‹ and known ‹ before You ‹ that it is our will ‹ to do ‹ Your will* «

וְלִשְׁקֹד עַל דַּלְתוֹתֶיךָ,*[2] כִּי טוֹב יוֹם בַּחֲצֵרֶיךָ מֵאָלֶף

and diligently to guard ‹ Your doorways,* « for ‹ better ‹ is one day ‹ in Your courtyards ‹ than a thousand ‹

בָּחַרְנוּ,*[3] וִירֵאִים וַחֲרֵדִים אֲנַחְנוּ מֵאֵימַת דִּינְךָ הַקָּדוֹשׁ.*

that is our choice.* « Fearful ‹ and terrified ‹ are we ‹ by the awe ‹ of Your sacred Judgment.* «

(1) *Berachos* 17a. (2) Cf. *Proverbs* 8:34. (3) Cf. *Psalms* 84:11.

10) alludes to the *filthy materialism* of which man strives to free himself. It is the trace of evil that lust leaves behind it. Such evil causes man to deceive himself and assign value to the empty temptations of material life.

גַּם אִסּוּר נִלְוֶה עִמָּם — *Also forbidden things joined with them.* This is a play on words based on *Psalms* 83:9: גַּם אַשּׁוּר נִלְוֶה עִמָּם; *even Assyria joined with them.*

The verse refers to the massive non-Jewish host that gathered to destroy Israel; in the context of the *Tashlich* prayer, the phrase refers to the host of temptations that influence man to sin.

אֲסוּרִים וּלְטוּשִׁים — *Forbidden yet burnished* [i.e., *gleamingly tempting*]. This is a play on words based on *Genesis* 25:3, where the progeny of Abraham and Keturah are listed: וּבְנֵי דְדָן הָיוּ אַשּׁוּרִם וּלְטוּשִׁם, *And the sons of Dedan were Ashurim and Letushim.*

In the context of this supplication, the word signifies that the evil inclination entices us to draw near to *proscribed* things that should be kept at a distance.

שֶׁרְצוֹנֵנוּ לַעֲשׂוֹת רְצוֹנְךָ — *That it is our will to do Your will.* At the conclusion of the *Shemoneh Esrei, R' Alexandri* would say, "Master of the universe, it is clearly evident to You that our wish is to fulfill Your wish, but what inhibits us? The yeast in the dough [i.e., the evil inclination that 'sours' us just as yeast sours dough" (*Rashi*)] (*Berachos* 17a).

וְלִשְׁקוֹד עַל דַּלְתוֹתֶיךָ — *And diligently to guard Your doorways.* This is based on *Proverbs* 8:34: אַשְׁרֵי אָדָם שֹׁמֵעַ לִי לִשְׁקֹד עַל דַּלְתֹתַי יוֹם יוֹם, *Praiseworthy is the man who hearkens to Me to guard* My *doorways* [i.e., the entrances to the House of Study] *diligently, day after day.*

כִּי טוֹב יוֹם בַּחֲצֵרֶיךָ מֵאָלֶף בָּחַרְנוּ — *For better is one day in Your courtyards than a thousand — that is our choice.* This is based on *Psalms* 84:11. It is far better to dwell in Your Presence [i.e., in the Temple] today and to die tomorrow than to live elsewhere [in exile] for one thousand years (*Targum; Rashi; Radak*).

[For in Your Presence, my spirit flourishes, but estranged from You, it withers.[1]]

Indeed, even one day of life in This World surpasses all of the existence in the World to Come (*Avos* 4:17), for This World is a *courtyard, where one prepares himself before entering the main hall,* the World to Come (*Avos* 4:16). Only in This World can man fulfill God's commandments and gain merits that will enrich his future reward. In the World to Come it is too late, for there man can but reap the fruits of what he planted in This World (*Alshich; Meir Tehillos*).

וִירֵאִים וַחֲרֵדִים אֲנַחְנוּ מֵאֵימַת דִּינְךָ הַקָּדוֹשׁ — *Fearful and terrified are we by the awe of Your sacred Judgment.* When R' Yochanan ben Zakkai was on his deathbed, his disciples

1. The Talmud (*Makkos* 10a) relates that David said to the Holy One, Blessed is He, "Sovereign of the universe, I overheard people saying, "When will this old man [i.e., David] die, so that his son Solomon may build the Temple and enable us to make the festival pilgrimage to that Holy Place?'" David rejoiced when he heard this [because it demonstrated how intensely the people yearned to serve God].

But God was not pleased. He said, "Far better a day in your courtyard than a thousand," i.e., a single day of David's devoted Torah study in My Presence surpasses the one thousand burnt-offerings that Solomon is destined to sacrifice before Me on the Temple Altar.

עַל כֵּן בָּאנוּ אֵלֶיךָ בִּכְפִיפַת רֹאשׁ וּנְמִיכַת קוֹמָה וַחֲלִישַׁת

‹ and exhausted ‹ posture ‹ humbled ‹ heads, ‹ with bowed « to You, ‹ we come ‹ Therefore

חֵיל לְהַזְכִּיר וּלְעוֹרֵר רַחֲמֶיךָ.

« Your mercy. ‹ and arouse ‹ to invoke « strength,

וִיהִי רָצוֹן מִלְּפָנֶיךָ, יהוה אֱלֹהַי וֵאלֹהֵי אֲבוֹתַי, אֵל

‹ God, « of my forefathers, ‹ and the God ‹ my God ‹ HASHEM, « before You, ‹ the will ‹ May it be

עֶלְיוֹן, מֻכְתָּר בִּתְלֵיסַר מְכִילִין דְּרַחֲמֵי, שֶׁתְּהֵא שָׁעָה

‹ that this moment be « of Mercy, ‹ Attributes ‹ with thirteen ‹ Who is crowned « the most High,

זוֹ עֵת רָצוֹן לְפָנֶיךָ, וְתִהְיֶה עוֹלָה לְפָנֶיךָ קְרִיאַת

‹ — [our] recital « before You ‹ rise up ‹ and may it « before You, ‹ of favor ‹ a time

שְׁלֹשׁ עֶשְׂרֵה מִדּוֹת שֶׁל רַחֲמִים שֶׁבִּפְסוּקִים: מִי אֵל

‹ *is a God* ‹ *Who* « that are found in the verses, ‹ Mercy ‹ of ‹ Attributes ‹ of the Thirteen

כָּמוֹךָ וְגוֹ׳,״[1] הַמְּכֻוָּנִים אֶל שְׁלֹשׁ עֶשְׂרֵה מִדּוֹת: אֵל רַחוּם

‹ *Compassionate* ‹ *God,* ‹ Attributes, ‹ the Thirteen ‹ to ‹ which correspond « *like You...,*

וְחַנּוּן וְגוֹ׳,״[2] אֲשֶׁר קָרֵינוּ לְפָנֶיךָ, כְּאִלּוּ הִשַּׂגְנוּ כָּל הַסּוֹדוֹת

‹ the mysteries ‹ all ‹ as if we had comprehended « before You, ‹ we have recited ‹ which « *and Gracious...,*

וְצֵרוּפֵי שֵׁמוֹת הַיּוֹצְאִים מֵהֶם,* וְזִוּוּגֵי מִדּוֹתֵיהֶם, אֲשֶׁר

‹ which ‹ of their Attributes, ‹ and the union « from them,* ‹ that emanate ‹ and the combinations of the [Holy] Names

(1) *Micah* 7:18. (2) *Exodus* 34:6.

---

visited him. As soon as he saw them he burst into tears. When they asked him why, he replied:

"Were I to be brought before a mortal king — who is here today but in the grave tomorrow, who may become angry with me, but whose anger is not everlasting, who may imprison me, but whose imprisonment is not forever, who may kill me, but who can kill only for this world, and who may be bribed — even then I would fear! But now I am led before the King of Kings, the Holy One, Blessed is He, who lives through all eternity, [should I not tremble before this awesome judgment]? If He is angry at me, His anger is everlasting; if He imprisons me, it is imprisonment forever; if He kills someone, that person is dead forever; and I can neither appease Him with words nor bribe Him with money. Moreover, there are two paths before me — one leading to Gan Eden and one leading to Gehinnom — and I know not through which I am to be led. Should I not weep?" (*Berachos* 28b).

וִיהִי רָצוֹן / May it be desirable.

וְתִהְיֶה עוֹלָה לְפָנֶיךָ ... כְּאִלּוּ הִשַּׂגְנוּ כָּל הַסּוֹדוֹת וְצֵרוּפֵי שֵׁמוֹת הַקְּדוֹשִׁים הַיּוֹצְאִים מֵהֶם — *May You*

אֶחָד בְּאֶחָד יִגָּשׁוּ*[1] לְהַמְתִּיק הַדִּינִים תַּקִּיפִים,* וְתַשְׁלִיךְ

one / to the other / come together,* / sweetening / the judgments / that are harsh.* / And [so] may You cast

בִּמְצוּלוֹת יָם כָּל חַטֹּאתֵינוּ.[2] וְאַתָּה בְּטוּבְךָ תְּעוֹרֵר רַחֲמֶיךָ

into the depths of the sea / all / our sins. / May You / in Your goodness / arouse / Your mercy

וְנִהְיֶה נְקִיִּים מִכָּל טֻמְאָה וְחֶלְאָה וְזֻהֲמָא, וְיַעֲלוּ

so that we may be / cleansed / of all / contamination, / filth, / and defilement. / May they arise

כָּל נִיצוֹצֵי הַקְּדֻשָּׁה אֲשֶׁר נִתְפַּזְּרוּ, וְיִתְבָּרְרוּ וְיִתְלַבְּנוּ[3]

— all / the sparks / of holiness / that / were scattered — / and be clarified / and whitened

בְּמִדַּת טוּבְךָ,* אַתָּה אֵל יְשׁוּעָתֵנוּ[4] נֹצֵר חֶסֶד לָאֲלָפִים.[5]

through Your Attribute of Goodness.* / You / are the God of our salvation, / Preserver of kindness / for thousands [of generations].

(1) *Job* 41:8. (2) Cf. *Micah* 7:19. (3) *Daniel* 12:10. (4) Cf. *Isaiah* 12:2. (5) *Exodus* 34:7.

---

consider [lit., *may it rise before You*] . . . *as if we had comprehended all of the mysteries and the combinations of the [Holy] Names that emanate from them.*

Ramban explains in his introduction to the Torah that the letters of the Torah can be divided to form different words than those to which we have become accustomed. By so doing, innumerable Names of God — both those known to us and His hidden, mystical ones — can be formed. Thus, when we read our text of the Torah, we are actually reading much more than the words we pronounce. We also read concealed ideas and combinations of letters that form various Names of God.

וְזִווּגֵי מִדּוֹתֵיהֶם אֲשֶׁר אֶחָד בְּאֶחָד יִגָּשׁוּ — *And the union of their Attributes which one to the other come together.*

As explained above, the Thirteen Attributes listed in *Exodus* correspond to the Thirteen Attributes enumerated by the prophet Micah.

לְהַמְתִּיק הַדִּינִים תַּקִּיפִים — *Sweetening the judgments that are harsh.* Even after the Heavenly Tribunal issues a sentence against the sinner, it is possible to "soften" the blow.[1]

וְיַעֲלוּ כָּל נִיצוֹצוֹת הַקְּדוּשָׁה אֲשֶׁר נִתְפַּזְּרוּ וְיִתְבָּרְרוּ וְיִתְלַבְּנוּ בְּמִדַּת טוּבְךָ — *May they arise — all the sparks of holiness that were scattered — and be clarified and whitened through Your Attribute of Goodness.* The purpose of every object, molecule, and atom, is to bring glory to God's Name. This potential to glorify God — the נִיצוֹץ קָדוֹשׁ, *holy spark* — rests concealed and dormant within an object until someone performs a meritorious action with it.

Even a profane article possesses the potential to sanctify God's Name and challenges man to do so. If he is successful, he redeems the spark in this unclean object (*Michtav MeEliyahu*, Vol. II, p. 255).

R' *Chaim of Volozhin* comments that the life-giving force of any food is the Divine spark within it. That spark emanates from

1. On Rosh Hashanah and Yom Kippur, mankind is judged and sentenced. The verdicts may sometimes be very harsh, but God still offers an opportunity for mercy. Immediately following these Days of Awe, the Jew is "exiled" from his home into the *succah*, because exile is a source of atonement for sin. If rain prevents him from entering the *succah*, however, it is an indication that God refuses to allow him atonement for the verdict of the Days of Judgment. This is the allegorical deeper meaning of the Mishnah (*Succah* 1:9) that speaks of a master who splashes water in the face of a servant who offers him wine (*Vilna Gaon*).

וּבְרֹב רַחֲמֶיךָ תִּתֶּן לָנוּ חַיִּים אֲרֻכִּים,* חַיִּים שֶׁל

‹ of ‹ a life ‹‹ that is long,* ‹ life ‹ us ‹ grant ‹‹ In Your abundant mercy,

שָׁלוֹם,* חַיִּים שֶׁל טוֹבָה,* חַיִּים שֶׁל בְּרָכָה, חַיִּים

‹ a life ‹‹ blessing,* ‹ of ‹ a life ‹‹ goodness,* ‹ of ‹ a life ‹‹ peace,*

שֶׁל פַּרְנָסָה טוֹבָה,* חַיִּים שֶׁל חִלּוּץ עֲצָמוֹת,* חַיִּים

‹ a life ‹‹ physical health,* ‹ of ‹ a life ‹‹ good sustenance,* ‹ of

שֶׁיֵּשׁ בָּהֶם יִרְאַת שָׁמַיִם וְיִרְאַת חֵטְא,* חַיִּים שֶׁאֵין בָּהֶם

‹ in which there is no ‹ a life ‹‹ of sin,* ‹ and fear ‹ of Heaven ‹ fear ‹ in which there is

---

God's utterance, *Let grain spring forth from the earth* (*Genesis* 1:11). When a person recites a blessing over his food, he releases the Divine spark, the spiritual energy hidden in the food. This holy force sustains life (*Ruach Chaim*).

וּבְרוֹב רַחֲמֶיךָ תִּתֶּן לָנוּ חַיִּים אֲרוּכִּים — *In Your abundant mercy, grant us life that is long.* Beginning with this request for long life until the conclusion of this section, the supplication quotes verbatim from the prayer of Rav, the foremost Talmudic sage of his era. He was accustomed to recite it daily upon the conclusion of his daily prayer (*Berachos* 16b), and it has been adopted as part of the liturgy in the prayer for the new month.

A careful study of this supplication reveals that everything Rav included here reflects his personal values and the events of his life.

חַיִּים שֶׁל שָׁלוֹם — *A life of peace.* In his personal dealings, Rav pursued peace and harmony under all circumstances. The Talmud (*Yoma* 87a) relates that a certain butcher mistreated Rav and quarreled with him. When the eve of the Day of Atonement arrived, the butcher did not come to ask Rav for forgiveness. "If he does not come to me," said Rav, "then I shall go to him to ask forgiveness!" On the road, R' Huna met Rav and inquired of him, "Where is the Master going?" "I am going to appease that man," Rav replied. "The Master is on his way to kill the man," remarked Rav Huna. [Knowing that the butcher would refuse Rav's overture, R' Huna was sure that he would be sorely punished.]

When Rav arrived at the shop, the butcher was cleaning the head of a cow. The butcher noticed Rav and said, "Is that you? Go away, for I want no dealings with you!" When the butcher resumed cleaning the cow's head, a bone splinter flew up striking him in the head and killing him.

חַיִּים שֶׁל טוֹבָה — *A life of goodness.* This refers to the life in which a man has the opportunity to enjoy every gift that God bestows. As Rav taught, possessions are meant to be used wisely and properly; not to be hoarded for some future that may never come (*Eruvin* 54a).

חַיִּים שֶׁל פַּרְנָסָה טוֹבָה — *A life of good sustenance. Good sustenance* does not mean one that provides riches; it means an independent livelihood that frees a man from envy of others and from dependence on them. Rav said, "When a man yearns for the table [i.e., the provisions and livelihood] of another man, the world becomes dark for him" (*Beitzah* 32b).

חַיִּים שֶׁל חִלּוּץ עֲצָמוֹת — *A life of physical health* [lit., *a life of release of the bones*]. This blessing is based on the words of the prophet: וְעַצְמֹתֶיךָ יַחֲלִיץ וְהָיִיתָ כְּגַן רָוֶה וּכְמוֹצָא מַיִם אֲשֶׁר לֹא יְכַזְּבוּ מֵימָיו, *And He will invigorate your bones, and you will be like a lush garden, and a water spring whose waters never cease to flow* (*Isaiah* 58:11).

The Talmud (*Yevamos* 102b) declares that one of the greatest blessings is robust health and vigor.

R' Yochanan testified that Rav came from a family well-known for its good health and strength (*Chullin* 84a).

חַיִּים שֶׁיֵּשׁ בָּהֶם יִרְאַת שָׁמַיִם וְיִרְאַת חֵטְא — *A life in which there is fear of Heaven and fear of sin.* The text in *Berachos* 16b mentions only יִרְאַת חֵטְא; later the words יִרְאַת שָׁמַיִם were inserted. This addition teaches that genuine *fear of sin* is *based on fear of Heaven.*

R' *Avrohom Abba Kaplan* explains that the

בּוּשָׁה וּכְלִמָּה, חַיִּים שֶׁל עֹשֶׁר וְכָבוֹד* לַעֲבוֹדָתֶךָ, חַיִּים

‹ a life « for Your service, ‹ and honor* ‹ wealth ‹ of ‹ a life « or humiliation, ‹ shame

שֶׁתְּהֵא בָנוּ אַהֲבַת תּוֹרָה* וְיִרְאַת שָׁמַיִם,* חַיִּים שֶׁתְּמַלֵּא

‹ in which You fulfill ‹ a life « of Heaven,* ‹ and fear ‹ of Torah* ‹ love ‹ in us ‹ in which there will be

כָּל מִשְׁאֲלוֹת לִבֵּנוּ לְטוֹבָה,*[1] וְזָכְרֵנוּ לְחַיִּים מֶלֶךְ חָפֵץ

‹ Who desires ‹ O King ‹ for life, ‹ Remember us « for the good.* ‹ of our heart ‹ the requests ‹ all

בַּחַיִּים, וְכָתְבֵנוּ בְּסֵפֶר הַחַיִּים, לְמַעַנְךָ אֱלֹהִים חַיִּים,[2]

« O Living God. ‹ — for Your sake, « of Life ‹ in the Book ‹ and inscribe us « life,

וּקְרַע רֹעַ גְּזַר דִּינֵנוּ,[3] וְיִקָּרְאוּ לְפָנֶיךָ זְכֻיּוֹתֵינוּ.

« our merits. ‹ before You ‹ And may there be read « of the decree of our judgment. ‹ the evil ‹ Tear up

(1) See *Berachos* 16b. (2) Addition to *Shemoneh Esrei* during Days of Awe. (3) *Avinu Malkeinu.*

more beloved an object, the greater the owner's fear lest it be damaged. Similarly, the more a person treasures *Heaven* — i.e., God — the more he is afraid to sin, lest he ruin the special relationship he enjoys with God.

חַיִּים שֶׁל עֹשֶׁר וְכָבוֹד — *A life of wealth and honor.* The *Chofetz Chaim* asked, "How can we request honor, since we know that the pursuit of honor and acclaim is most despicable trait?" We seek riches only in order to bring glory to the Jewish people as a whole, but not for ourselves. Similarly, in the liturgy of the *Yamim Nora'im* we pray, וּבְכֵן תֵּן כָּבוֹד ה׳ לְעַמֶּךָ, *And thus, grant honor, Hashem, to Your nation.*

The Talmud (*Berachos* 57b) relates that Rav was a man of wealth. Rav knew that prosperity brings its possessor dignity and honor, yet, the rich man must take care not to become overly proud and arrogant.

Accordingly, we ask for *prosperity* coupled with the real *honor,* which comes when wealth and status are used properly in God's service, without resulting in vanity and arrogance.

In addition, the rich man should strive to bring *honor* to himself by giving charity with his riches. Rav said, "The rich men of Babylonia will someday inherit an estate in Gehinnom." [This is because they lack mercy and give no charity (*Rashi*)] (*Beitzah* 32b).

חַיִּים שֶׁתְּהֵא בָנוּ אַהֲבַת תּוֹרָה — *A life in which there will be in us love of Torah.* Rav's insatiable love of Torah is reflected in his statement: "A person should never refrain from attending the House of Study even for a moment [lest, during his absence, he miss an important lesson]" (*Shabbos* 83b).

A few phrases earlier, the wording is חַיִּים שֶׁיֵּשׁ בָּהֶם, *a life in which there is. . .,* but now the prayer reads חַיִּים שֶׁתְּהֵא בָנוּ, *a life in which there will be in us.* First we ask for the externals — the outer lifestyle of the Jew. Now we request deeper meaning, inner commitment and sincerity. This can be accomplished only through love of Torah and its study.

וְיִרְאַת שָׁמַיִם — *And fear of Heaven.* Actually, these words are a repetition of an earlier request for יִרְאַת שָׁמַיִם. *Chofetz Chaim* explains that since we subsequently ask for a *life of prosperity and honor* — which can pose a grave threat to one's character by fostering arrogance and the defiance of God — a *second* plea for *fear of sin* is required.

חַיִּים שֶׁתְּמַלֵּא כָּל מִשְׁאֲלוֹת לִבֵּנוּ לְטוֹבָה — *A life in which You fulfill all the requests of our heart for the good.* Not always are a man's desires truly in his best interest; he may very well yearn for something harmful. Therefore, upon completing this list of requests, we ask

אֵל מָלֵא רַחֲמִים,* יֶהֱמוּ נָא רַחֲמֶיךָ לְקַבֵּל בְּרָצוֹן

‹ so that You may accept favorably ‹ be Your compassion ‹ may aroused, please, « of mercy,* ‹ full ‹ God,

הַכְנָעָתֵנוּ וְהַרְהוֹרֵי תְשׁוּבָה הַמִּתְנוֹצְצִים בָּנוּ, בְּשַׁגַּם[1] לִבֵּנוּ

‹ as our heart ‹ Now, inasmuch « within us. ‹ that flash ‹ of repentance ‹ and our thoughts ‹ our submission

אָטוּם סָתוּם וְחָתוּם, לֹא אִתָּנוּ יוֹדֵעַ זוֹ הִיא בִּיאָה זוֹ הִיא

‹ what is [true] ‹ *coming forth* [toward You] ‹ what is [true] ‹ knows ‹ among us ‹ and no one « and sealed, ‹ closed, ‹ is blocked,

שִׁיבָה,[2]* מָה אָנוּ וּמָה בָּאנוּ לְתַקֵּן. רַב לְהוֹשִׁיעַ, הָאֵר עֵינֵינוּ

‹ enlighten our eyes « [Therefore,] You, Who are abundantly able to save, « to rectify. ‹ are we *coming forth* ‹ and what ‹ are we ‹ what « *returning* [to You],*

כַּאֲשֶׁר בְּגֹדֶל רַחֲמֶיךָ הִבְטַחְתָּנוּ: פִּתְחוּ לִי פֶּתַח כְּחֻדּוֹ

‹ *as [tiny as] the point* ‹ *an entrance* ‹ *for Me* ‹ *Open* « You promised us: ‹ mercy, ‹ in Your great ‹ as,

שֶׁל מַחַט, וַאֲנִי אֶפְתַּח לָכֶם פֶּתַח כְּפִתְחוֹ שֶׁל אוּלָם,*[3]

« *the Temple Sanctuary.** ‹ *of* ‹ *as [large as] the entrance* ‹ *an entrance* ‹ *for You* ‹ *will open* ‹ *and I* « *a needle,* ‹ *of*

(1) *Genesis* 6:3. (2) See *Eruvin* 51a. (3) See *Shir HaShirim Rabbah* 5:3.

---

that they be fulfilled in a manner that is not detrimental (*Rashash* to *Berachos* 16b).

אֵל מָלֵא רַחֲמִים / God, full of Mercy.

This supplication captures the humility and submissiveness of a people eternally loyal and devoted to the Creator. Israel is helpless without God's assistance, but it recognizes that it is unworthy of His aid. Israel claims for itself only one merit: throughout the millennia, millions of its sons and daughters have martyred themselves to sanctify His Name. Israel asks God to grant His people the opportunity to consecrate God's Name in life rather than in death.

זוֹ הִיא שִׁיבָה זוֹ הִיא בִּיאָה — *What is [true] coming forth [toward You], what is [true] returning [to You].* [Alternatively: *How to approach You or how to return to You.*] This Talmudic phrase [found in *Eruvin* 51a; *Niddah* 22b] is based on *Leviticus* 14:39, 44, which speaks of the priest who checks the leprous sign on the stones of a house.

Scripture here implies that one needs an expert to scrutinize a sign of sin and defilement; but we, in our degradation, lack an expert who can reveal to us where our faults lie.

פִּתְחוּ לִי פֶּתַח כְּחוּדוֹ שֶׁל מַחַט, וַאֲנִי אֶפְתַּח לָכֶם פֶּתַח כְּפִתְחוֹ שֶׁל אוּלָם — *Open for Me an entrance as tiny as the point of a needle, and I, in turn, will open for you an entrance as large as the entrance of the Temple Sanctuary.*

The source of this exact quotation is unknown. A similar version in *Shir HaShirim Rabbah* 5:3, reads: פִּתְחוּ לִי פֶּתַח אֶחָד שֶׁל תְּשׁוּבָה כְּחוּדָהּ שֶׁל מַחַט וַאֲנִי פּוֹתֵחַ לָכֶם פְּתָחִים שֶׁיִּהְיוּ עֲגָלוֹת וּקְרוֹנוֹת נִכְנָסוֹת, *Make Me a single opening of repentance like the point of a needle. Then I will provide you with entrances that wagons and carriages can enter.*

The Mishnah (*Middos* 3:7) states that the width of the entranceway of the אוּלָם, *hall,* was twenty cubits and its height was forty cubits. The *Gerrer Rebbe* noted that this entranceway was unique not only because of its size but also because it had no doors [see *Eruvin* 3b]. Thus, God promised Israel that

וּרְאֵה כִּי אָזְלַת יָד וְאֶפֶס עָצוּר וְעָזוּב.[1]* וְאֵין חוֹנֵן

〈 There is no one who shows favor 《 or strengthened.* 〈 saved 〈 and there is no one 《 is [our] power, 〈 gone 〈 that 〈 See

וְאֵין מְרַחֵם זוּלָתֶךָ, כִּי חֲנוּנֶיךָ הֵם חֲנוּנִים וּמְרֻחָמֶיךָ

《 and those to whom You are merciful 《 are favored; 〈 —[only] they 《 for those whom You favor, 《 except for You, 〈 who shows mercy 〈 and no one

הֵם מְרֻחָמִים, כִּדְכְתִיב: וְחַנֹּתִי אֶת אֲשֶׁר אָחֹן וְרִחַמְתִּי

〈 *and I will be merciful* 〈 *I will favor* 〈 *to those whom* 〈 *I will show favor* 《 as it is written: 《 — [only] they are treated mercifully;

אֶת אֲשֶׁר אֲרַחֵם.[2]* וּבְכֵן, לֵב טָהוֹר בְּרָא לָנוּ אֱלֹהִים* וְרוּחַ

〈 and a spirit 《 O God,* 〈 for us, 〈 create 〈 that is pure 〈 a heart 《 And so, 《 *I will treat mercifully.** 〈 *to those whom*

נָכוֹן חַדֵּשׁ בְּקִרְבֵּנוּ,[3]* וְרִשְׁפֵּי הִתְעוֹרְרוּת לִבֵּנוּ בְּאַהֲבָתֶךָ

〈 in Your love 〈 of our heart 〈 of arousal 〈 The flames 《 within us.* 〈 renew 〈 that is steadfast

(1) *Deuteronomy* 32:36. (2) *Exodus* 33:19. (3) Cf. *Psalms* 51:12.

if they would repent even slightly, He would keep the entrance of repentance [*teshuvah*] open for them at all times.

R' Yisrael Salanter compares repentance to needlepoint. He notes that although the hole made in needlepoint is tiny, it is penetrating, for it pierces the fabric completely and draws a thread behind it. Similarly, God welcomes repentance, even if the penitent rectifies only one tiny sin, if his repentance for that transgression is complete and sincere. *R' Salanter* explains that if true contrition penetrates the depth of a man's heart, then it will draw in its wake much more genuine penitence.

וּרְאֵה כִּי אָזְלַת יָד וְאֶפֶס עָצוּר וְעָזוּב — *See that gone is our power and there* is *no one saved or strengthened [Deuteronomy* 32:36]. Earlier, Scripture says that God will judge Israel harshly for their sins. He will, however, take pity on them when He sees that they are utterly helpless and leaderless. If they turn to Him at that time — even if they are motivated primarily by desperation — God will accept their repentance.

וְחַנֹּתִי אֶת אֲשֶׁר אָחֹן, וְרִחַמְתִּי אֶת אֲשֶׁר אֲרַחֵם — *I will show favor to those whom I will favor, and I will be merciful to those whom I will treat mercifully (Exodus* 33:19). *Maharil Diskin* (commentary to *Parshas Vayishlach)* explains that God's blessing can sometimes become a curse. God knows that if some people are granted prosperity, they will become arrogant and defy God, or they will use their wealth to destroy their rivals and opponents. God knows that if He is compassionate to such people, He will eventually have to withdraw His compassion and unleash His wrath. Therefore, God is compassionate only to those who will benefit and improve from His bounty and to whom He can continue to show compassion and mercy.

[This explains the preceding words of supplication: כִּי חֲנוּנֶיךָ הֵמָּה חֲנוּנִים, *Because those to whom You show favor, only they are favored.*]

לֵב טָהוֹר בְּרָא לָנוּ אֱלֹהִים — *A heart that is pure create for us, O God.* This is based on *Psalms* 51:12: *A pure heart create for me, O God, and a steadfast spirit renew within me.* David composed this psalm when Nathan the prophet came to chastise him for his relationship with Bat-sheva (see *Psalms* 51:2). David humbly accepted the rebuke and dedicated his entire being to wholehearted repentance.

וְרוּחַ נָכוֹן חַדֵּשׁ בְּקִרְבֵּנוּ — *And a spirit that is steadfast renew within us. Sforno* renders נָכוֹן as synonymous with מוּכָן, *prepared.* David pleaded, "Grant me an intellectual

וּבְתוֹרָתֶךָ יַתְמִידוּ וְיִתְרַבּוּ בְּלִי הֶפְסֵק. עָזְרֵנוּ אֱלֹהֵי

and in Your Torah — may they continue constantly and increase without interruption. Assist us, O God

יִשְׁעֵנוּ עַל דְּבַר כְּבוֹד שְׁמֶךָ,[1] תָּחֵל שָׁנָה וּבִרְכוֹתֶיהָ.*

of our salvation, for the sake of the glory of Your Name. May the new year begin and its blessings.*

וּתְזַכֵּנוּ שֶׁיְּהֵא לִבֵּנוּ נָכוֹן וּמָסוּר בְּיָדֵינוּ, וְלֹא נִכְעַס וְלֹא

Grant us the merit that our heart should be steadfast and subject to our control, neither should we get angry nor

נַכְעִיסֶךָ, וְתַסְפִּיק בְּיָדֵינוּ לְהִתְרַחֵק מִכָּל הַמִּדּוֹת הָרָעוֹת

make You angry. Provide us with the ability to distance ourselves from all traits that are immoral

וְהָאֲסוּרוֹת, וּבִפְרָט זַכֵּנוּ לְהִתְרַחֵק מֵהַגַּאֲוָה וְהַכַּעַס

and forbidden, and in particular, grant us the merit to distance ourselves from arrogance, anger,

וְהַהַקְפָּדָה וְכָל גֹּבַהּ לֵב, וְנִהְיֶה מְיֻשָּׁבִים בְּדַעְתֵּנוּ וְנַכִּיר

being overly strict with others, and all haughtiness. May we be settled in our minds. May we recognize

מִעוּט עֶרְכֵּנוּ, וְנַפְשֵׁנוּ כֶּעָפָר לַכֹּל תִּהְיֶה,* וְלֹא נִתְכַּעֵס

the paltriness of our worth. Let our souls like dust to everyone be.* Let us not be angered

וְלֹא נַקְפִּיד, וְנִהְיֶה אֹהֲבֵי שָׁלוֹם וּמַרְבִּים שָׁלוֹם, וּבְצֵל

nor overly strict with others; and let us be lovers of peace and promoters of peace; and in the shadow

כְּנָפֶיךָ נֶחֱסֶה, וּתְזַכֵּנוּ לְהִתְרַחֵק מִלֵּיצָנוּת וְשֶׁקֶר וַחֲנֻפָּה

of Your wing shelter us. Grant us the merit to distance ourselves from scorning, falsehood, flattery,

וְלָשׁוֹן הָרָע, וְדִבּוּר חֹל בְּשַׁבָּת, וְכָל דִּבּוּר אָסוּר, וִיהִי

gossip, speaking about weekday matters on the Sabbath, and all [other] speech that is forbidden. May

(1) *Psalms* 79:9.

spirit capable of understanding God's ways and equipped to communicate these insights to others."

תָּחֵל שָׁנָה וּבִרְכוֹתֶיהָ — *May the New Year begin and its blessings.* This alludes to *Megillah* 31b, which teaches that the annual cycle of Sabbath Torah reading is designed so that all the curses enumerated in *Deuteronomy* will be read before Rosh Hashanah.

וְנַפְשֵׁנוּ כֶּעָפָר לַכֹּל תִּהְיֶה — *Let our souls like dust to everyone be.* This is based on the words that *Mar bar Ravina* would say after concluding the *Amidah* service (see *Berachos* 17a).

The commentators explain that although people constantly trample the dust and the

רֹב דִּבּוּרֵנוּ בַּתּוֹרָה וּבְסֵדֶר וְאֹפֶן עֲבוֹדָתְךָ עֲבוֹדַת

‹ the service « of Your service, ‹ and manner ‹ and the form ‹ be about Torah ‹ of our conversation ‹ the majority

הַקֹּדֶשׁ, וּתְאַזְּרֵנוּ חַיִל לִשְׁמֹר לְפִינוּ מֵחֵטְא בִּלְשׁוֹנֵנוּ.

« with our tongue. ‹ from sinning ‹ our mouths ‹ to restrain ‹ with strength ‹ Gird us « of holiness.

אָב הָרַחֲמָן, תֵּן בָּנוּ כֹּחַ וּבְרִיאוּת, וְזַכֵּנוּ לְהִתְרַחֵק

‹ to distance ourselves ‹ Grant us the merit « and health. ‹ strength ‹ us ‹ Give « Who is merciful! ‹ Father

מִתַּאֲוַת תַּעֲנוּגֵי וְהֶבְלֵי הָעוֹלָם הַזֶּה, וְנֹאכַל לְשֹׂבַע

‹ [only] to satisfy ‹ May we eat « of This World. ‹ and futilities ‹ for the pleasures ‹ from desire

נַפְשֵׁנוּ, וְכֵן בְּכָל צְרָכֵינוּ יִהְיוּ כָּל מַעֲשֵׂינוּ לְשֵׁם שָׁמָיִם.

« of Heaven. ‹ be for the sake ‹ our actions ‹ all ‹ — may « our needs ‹ regarding all ‹ and similarly « our souls,

וּתְזַכֵּנוּ לִהְיוֹת שְׂמֵחִים בְּעֵסֶק תּוֹרָתְךָ וּבְמִצְוֹתֶיךָ, וְלִהְיוֹת

‹ and to have « and Your commandments, ‹ with Your Torah ‹ in [our] involvement ‹ joyful ‹ to be ‹ Grant us the merit

בִּטְחוֹנֵנוּ בְּךָ תָּדִיר, וְיִהְיֶה לָנוּ לֵב שָׂמֵחַ לַעֲבוֹדָתֶךָ.

« in Your service. ‹ that is joyful ‹ a heart ‹ and may we have « always, ‹ in You ‹ our trust

אָנָּא מֶלֶךְ רַחוּם וְחַנּוּן, הַנְּשָׁמָה לָךְ וְהַגּוּף פָּעֳלָךְ,

« is Your work; ‹ and the body ‹ is Yours ‹ — the soul « and compassionate ‹ merciful ‹ O King, ‹ Please,

חוּסָה עַל עֲמָלָךְ.[1] וּבְכֵן יֶהֱמוּ נָא רַחֲמֶיךָ[2] עָלֵינוּ, וּתְזַכֵּנוּ

‹ and grant us the merit « for us, ‹ Your compassion ‹ please may aroused be « And so, « Your labor! ‹ on ‹ have pity

לְהַשְׁלִים תִּקּוּן נֶפֶשׁ רוּחַ וּנְשָׁמָה בְּגִלְגּוּל זֶה וְלֹא

‹ so that we not « in this incarnation, ‹ and soul, ‹ spirit, ‹ of our life, ‹ the perfection ‹ to complete

נֹאבַד חַס וְשָׁלוֹם, וְתַשְׁפִּיעַ שֶׁפַע קֹדֶשׁ עַל נֶפֶשׁ רוּחַ

‹ spirit, ‹ our life, ‹ on ‹ of sanctity ‹ an outpouring ‹ May You cause to flow « Heaven forbid. « perish,

(1) *Shomei'a Tefillah — Selichos* for Days of Awe. (2) *Shemoneh Esrei* — עַל הַצַּדִּיקִים.

soil, it never refuses to give forth its produce to man. We pray that even when people offend and insult us, we will act generously toward them.

וּנְשָׁמָה לְהַתְמִיד בַּעֲבוֹדָתֶךָ וְלַעֲשׂוֹת רְצוֹנֵנוּ כִּרְצוֹנֶךָ[1]

« conform to Your will, ‹ our will ‹ in order to make ‹ in Your service, ‹ to continue constantly ‹ and soul,

כָּל יְמֵי חַיֵּינוּ, אֲנַחְנוּ וְזַרְעֵנוּ וְזֶרַע זַרְעֵנוּ, וּתְזַכֵּנוּ לַעֲסֹק

‹ to engage ‹ Grant us the merit « of our children. ‹ and the children ‹ our children, ‹ — [for] us, « of our lives ‹ the ‹ all days

בְּתוֹרָתְךָ הַקְּדוֹשָׁה לִשְׁמָהּ וּלְכַוֵּן לַאֲמִתָּהּ שֶׁל תּוֹרָה,

« the Torah. ‹ of ‹ and that [our study] be in accord with the true meaning « for its own sake, ‹ in [the study of] Your holy Torah

וְתַצִּיל מִלִּבֵּנוּ טָעוּת בַּהֲלָכָה וּבְהוֹרָאָה, וְאַל תַּצֵּל מִפִּינוּ

‹ from our mouth ‹ remove ‹ and do not « and in rendering decisions, ‹ in [determining the] halachah ‹ any error ‹ from our heart ‹ Remove

דְּבַר אֱמֶת[2] לְעוֹלָם. וְנִהְיֶה אֲנַחְנוּ וְצֶאֱצָאֵינוּ* וְצֶאֱצָאֵי

‹ and the offspring ‹ our offspring,* ‹ — we, « May we be « ever. ‹ of truth, ‹ the word

צֶאֱצָאֵינוּ כֻּלָּנוּ יוֹדְעֵי שְׁמֶךָ וְלוֹמְדֵי תוֹרָתֶךָ לִשְׁמָהּ[3]

« for its own sake, ‹ Your Torah ‹ and study ‹ Your Name ‹ people who know « all of us, « of our offspring —

וּמְקַיְּמֵי מִצְוֹתֶיךָ, וְלֹא יִמָּצֵא בָנוּ, וְלֹא בְזַרְעֵנוּ וְלֹא

‹ nor ‹ among our children, ‹ nor « among us, ‹ May there not be found « Your commandments. ‹ and fulfill

בְּזֶרַע זַרְעֵנוּ, שׁוּם פְּגַם וְשׁוּם פְּסוּל, וְלֹא יִתְחַלֵּל

‹ May there be no desecration « disqualification. ‹ or any ‹ defect ‹ any « of our children, ‹ among the children

שִׁמְךָ עַל יָדֵינוּ, חַס וְשָׁלוֹם.

« Heaven forbid. « through us, ‹ of Your Name

וּרְאֵה כִּי עַמְּךָ הַגּוֹי הַגָּדוֹל הַזֶּה,[4] זֶרַע אוֹהֲבֶיךָ,

‹ of Your beloved ones, ‹ the children « — this great nation, « it is Your people ‹ that ‹ See

אַבְרָהָם יִצְחָק וְיִשְׂרָאֵל עֲבָדֶיךָ בְּנֵי בְחוּנֶיךָ. וּבְגָלוּתָם

‹ And in their exile, « of Your tested ones. ‹ the children « Your servants; ‹ and Israel, ‹ Isaac, ‹ Abraham,

(1) Cf. *Avos* 2:4. (2) Cf. *Psalms* 119:43. (3) Cf. Blessing of the Torah. (4) Cf. *Exodus* 33:13.

וְנִהְיֶה אֲנַחְנוּ וְצֶאֱצָאֵינוּ — *May we be — we, our offspring* ... The ensuing lines are part of the text of the blessing over Torah study, as recorded in the Talmud (*Berachos* 11b).

וְדַלּוּתָם וְשִׁפְלוּתָם וְלַחֲצָם וְדָחְקָם זֶה כַּמָּה מֵאוֹת שָׁנִים

their poverty, / their downtrodden state, / their oppression, / and their repression / now / several / hundred / years,

קוֹרְאִים בִּשְׁמֶךָ, וּמַאֲמִינִים בְּךָ וּבְתוֹרָתֶךָ, וְכַמָּה אֲלָפִים

they call out / in Your Name / and believe / in You / and Your Torah. / Many / thousands

וּרְבָבוֹת מָסְרוּ עַצְמָן לַהֲרִיגָה וְלִשְׂרֵפָה עַל קְדֻשַּׁת שְׁמֶךָ.

and tens of thousands / have given up / their [lives] / to murder / and immolation / for / the sanctification / of Your Name.

נָא גִבּוֹר דּוֹרְשֵׁי יִחוּדְךָ כְּבָבַת שָׁמְרֵם.*[1] וְתִתְמַלֵּא רַחֲמִים

Please, O Strong One / — those who seek / Your Oneness, / like the pupil of an eye / guard them.* / Be full / of mercy

עַל כָּל אַחֵינוּ בֵּית יִשְׂרָאֵל* הַנְּפוֹצִים בְּאַרְבַּע כַּנְפוֹת

upon / all / our brethren, / the Children / of Israel,* / who are scattered / throughout the four / corners

הָאָרֶץ, וּבִפְרָט עַל יוֹשְׁבֵי אֶרֶץ יִשְׂרָאֵל, וְעַל יוֹשְׁבֵי

of the earth; / and particularly / upon the inhabitants / of Eretz Yisrael, / upon the inhabitants

הָעִיר הַזֹּאת, וְעַל כָּל הַקָּהָל הַקָּדוֹשׁ הַזֶּה, וּתְרַחֵם עָלֵינוּ

of this city, / and upon / all / of this holy congregation. / Have mercy / upon us

וַעֲלֵיהֶם, וְתַצִּילֵנוּ מֵרָעָה וּמֵרָעָב וּמִשְּׁבִי וּבִזָּה וּמִכָּל חֵטְא,

and upon them, / and save us / from evil, / famine, / captivity, / plunder, / and from all / sin.

וְתִשְׁלַח רְפוּאָה שְׁלֵמָה לְכָל חוֹלֵי עַמְּךָ יִשְׂרָאֵל, אֵל נָא

Send / a healing / that is complete / to all / the sick / of Your people, / Israel. / O God, please,

---

(1) אָנָּא בְּכֹחַ.

נָא גִבּוֹר, דּוֹרְשֵׁי יִחוּדְךָ כְּבָבַת שָׁמְרֵם — *Please, O Strong One — those who seek Your Oneness, like the pupil of an eye guard them.*

This is the third line of the Kabbalistic poem אָנָּא בְּכֹחַ, which is attributed to the holy Tanna, *R' Nechunya ben HaKaneh.* It is based on God's secret, Holy Name of forty-two letters (*Kiddushin* 71a). This name is revealed only to people of rare holiness (*Tikkun Tefillah*).

All Jews seek the revelation of the Oneness of God's Name, for the Jewish nation is dedicated to teaching the world that God controls every phase of creation.

אַחֵינוּ בֵּית יִשְׂרָאֵל — *Our brethren, the Children of Israel.* The Talmud (*Berachos* 54b) teaches that there are four cases in which people are obligated to offer thanks to God for their salvation: (1) when a person returns safely from a sea voyage; (2) when someone crosses the desert unharmed; (3) when a person recovers from a serious illness and (4) when a person is released from prison. This supplication begs God to rescue the people whose lives are endangered by such perils. This prayer is most appropriate for Rosh Hashanah, when all lives hang in the balance and are judged by the

רְפָא נָא לָהֶם,*¹ וּתְקַיֵּם בְּכָל אֶחָד מֵהֶם מִקְרָא שֶׁכָּתוּב:

« that is written: ‹ the verse ‹ of them ‹ one ‹ for each ‹ Fulfill « them now!* ‹ heal

יהוה יִסְעָדֶנּוּ עַל עֶרֶשׂ דְּוָי,* כָּל מִשְׁכָּבוֹ הָפַכְתָּ בְחָלְיוֹ.*²

« *by his illness.* ‹ *You have upset* ‹ *[even when] all his restfulness* « *of misery,* ‹ *the bed* ‹ *on* ‹ *will fortify him* ‹ *HASHEM*

וְהַבְּרִיאִים מֵעַמְּךָ יִשְׂרָאֵל תַּתְמִיד בְּרִיאוּתָם* שֶׁלֹּא יֶחֱלוּ,

« that they not become ill, ‹ their health,* ‹ — sustain « Israel ‹ among Your people ‹ As for the healthy ones

חַס וְשָׁלוֹם. וְתַצִּילֵנוּ וְתַצִּיל לְכָל יִשְׂרָאֵל מִכָּל נֶזֶק,

«harm ‹ from all ‹ of Israel ‹ all ‹ and save ‹ Save us « Heaven forbid.

וּמִכָּל צַר וּמַשְׂטִין³ וּמְקַטְרֵג,* וּמֵרוּחַ רָעָה, וּמִדִּקְדּוּקֵי

‹ and from the pangs « of depression, ‹ from a spirit «and accuser,* ‹ adversary, ‹ foe, ‹ and from every

(1) Cf. *Numbers* 12:13. (2) *Psalms* 41:4. (3) Cf. *Avinu Malkeinu*.

Heavenly Tribunal.

אֵל נָא רְפָא נָא לָהֶם — *O God, please! Heal them, now!* This based on *Numbers* 12:13. When Miriam spoke disparagingly of her brother, Moses, she was afflicted with leprosy. Moses not only forgave her but prayed on her behalf, רְפָא נָא לָהּ, *heal her now.*

ה׳ יִסְעָדֶנּוּ עַל עֶרֶשׂ דְּוָי — *Hashem will fortify him on the bed of misery.* The Talmud (*Shabbos* 12b) derives from this verse that God supplies the invalid with strength and nutrition, and that the שְׁכִינָה, *Divine Presence*, rests at the head of every sick bed. Therefore, a visitor should not sit on an invalid's bed [for this would imply irreverence for the *Shechinah*].

כָּל מִשְׁכָּבוֹ הָפַכְתָּ בְחָלְיוֹ — *All his restfulness* [lit., *bedding*) *You have upset by his illness.* This translations follows *Rashi* and *Radak*, who interpret חָלְיוֹ as the most severe stage of *his illness* and מִשְׁכָּבוֹ as *his restfulness.*

Radak offers another interpretation: Despite the severity of the illness, You provided the invalid with the strength to turn from side to side on his bed.

וְהַבְּרִיאִים מֵעַמְּךָ יִשְׂרָאֵל, תַּתְמִיד בְּרִיאוּתָם — *As for the healthy ones among Your people, Israel, sustain their health.*

The Sages emphasize that even a slight ailment should not be taken lightly, because it is a sign of God's displeasure. If the warning is ignored, more serious maladies may follow.

A person should always implore Divine mercy that he not fall ill, because once he does become ill they [the heavenly forces] tell him, "Bring proof of your virtues and merits; only then will you be released!" If one senses even a slight headache he should feel like a prisoner placed in chains. If his health deteriorates to the point where he is confined to bed, he should consider himself like a person on trial for his life who can be saved only by the most powerful and influential defenders (*Shabbos* 32a).

וְתַצִּילֵנוּ . . . מִכָּל צַר וּמַשְׂטִין וּמְקַטְרֵג — *And save us from every foe, adversary, and accuser.*

The Talmud (*Bava Basra* 16b) teaches that all the diverse aspects of evil are really a single force cloaked in different guises. First, the יֵצֶר הָרַע, *evil inclination*, descends to earth to seduce a man to sin. Then the Evil One rises heavenward and appears before the Heavenly Tribunal as שָׂטָן הַמְקַטְרֵג, *the accusing prosecutor*, demanding punishment for the offender. Once a guilty verdict is issued, the Evil One is sent to earth as the מַלְאַךְ הַמָּוֶת, *the Angel of Death*, to carry out the Heavenly sentence.

The Rabbis taught that Satan exerts greater effort to accuse and harm a person who is in

עֲנִיּוּת,* וּמִכָּל מִינֵי פֻּרְעָנִיּוֹת הַמִּתְרַגְּשׁוֹת בָּעוֹלָם.[1]

« upon the world. ‹ that converge ‹ of misfortunes ‹ manner ‹ and from all « of poverty,*

וְתִפְקֹד בְּזֶרַע שֶׁל קַיָּמָא, זֶרַע קֹדֶשׁ, לְכָל חֲשׂוּכֵי בָנִים,

« of children. ‹ who are deprived ‹ to all « — holy offspring — « through granting children who survive ‹ Remember

וְהַיּוֹשְׁבוֹת עַל הַמַּשְׁבֵּר[2] תּוֹצִיא אוֹתָן מֵאֲפֵלָה לְאוֹרָה,

« to light, ‹ from darkness ‹ — remove them « And women who are in labor

וְיֵצֵא הַוָּלָד בְּשָׁעָה טוֹבָה, וְלֹא יֶאֱרַע שׁוּם צַעַר וְשׁוּם

‹ nor any ‹ pain ‹ any ‹ occur ‹ and may there not « that is opportune, ‹ at the time ‹ and let the infant emerge

נֶזֶק לֹא לַיּוֹלְדוֹת וְלֹא לְיַלְדֵיהֶן,* וְאַל יִמְשֹׁל אַסְכָּרָה

‹ — croup « hold sway ‹ Let these not « to their newborn infants.* ‹ nor ‹ to the women giving birth ‹ neither « harm,

וְשֵׁדִין* וְרוּחִין וְלִילִין לְכָל יַלְדֵי עַמְּךָ בֵּית יִשְׂרָאֵל,

« of Israel. ‹ the Children ‹ of Your people, ‹ over any of the young children « and various evil forces —*

וּתְגַדְּלֵם לְתוֹרָתֶךָ וּלְמִצְוֹתֶיךָ בְּחַיֵּי אֲבִיהֶם וְאִמָּם.

« and mothers. ‹ of their fathers ‹ in the lifetimes ‹ and Your commandments ‹ [to be faithful] to Your Torah ‹ Raise them

(1) Cf. Wayfarer's Prayer. (2) Lit., *sit upon the childbirth chair.*

---

danger (*Rashi, Genesis* 42:4; *Deuteronomy* 23:10).

However, at the very time of Satan's accusation, the angel Michael defends Israel and enumerates their many virtues and merits (*Shemos Rabbah* 18:5).

וּמֵרוּחַ רָעָה, וּמִדִּקְדּוּקֵי עֲנִיּוּת — *From a spirit of depression and from the pangs of poverty.*

The Rabbis taught that three things can pervert a man's mind and drive him away from God: idol worship, a melancholy spirit, and the pangs of dire poverty (*Eruvin* 41b).

וְהַיּוֹשְׁבוֹת עַל הַמַּשְׁבֵּר, תּוֹצִיאֵם מֵאֲפֵלָה לְאוֹרָה ... וְלֹא יֶאֱרַע שׁוּם צַעַר וָנֶזֶק, לֹא לַיּוֹלְדוֹת וְלֹא לְיַלְדֵיהֶן — *And women who are in labor — remove them from darkness to light... and may there not occur any pain nor any harm neither to the women giving birth nor to their newborn infants.* The Mishnah (*Shabbos* 2:6) teaches that women sometimes die in childbirth as punishment for their sins. The Talmud (*Shabbos* 32a) notes that when a woman is physically healthy, even relatively minor merits can protect her; at childbirth, however, the danger is so great that only a miracle can save her life. At that time, her sins may render her unworthy of Divine assistance (see *Rashi, Shabbos* 32a s.v. אַבַּב חוּטְרָא מִילֵי).

וְאַל יִמְשׁוֹל אַסְכָּרָה וְשֵׁדִין — *Let these not hold sway — croup and various evil forces.*

According to the Talmud (*Berachos* 8a), there are nine hundred and three ways of dying. The most difficult of all is croup, which is likened to a sharp thorn stuck in a ball of wool. The wool becomes entangled with the thorn; any attempt to free the thorn tears the wool. The Talmud (*Shabbos* 33a) says that an attack of croup is punishment for לָשׁוֹן הָרַע, *slander.* [Since a person who slanders others misuses his throat and vocal chords, he is afflicted with croup, which affects precisely those parts of the body that were involved in his sin.]

וּבְנֵי יִשְׂרָאֵל עַמְּךָ יוֹרְדֵי הַיָּם,[1] פְּצֵם וְהַצִּילֵם מִמַּיִם רַבִּים

As for the members of Israel ‹ Your people ‹ who go down ‹ to the sea « release them — › and rescue them ‹ from great waters, «

מִיַּד בְּנֵי נֵכָר,[2] הַצִּילֵם מִטִּיט וְאַל יִטְבָּעוּ, יִנָּצְלוּ מִשְּׁאוֹנָם

[and] from the hand of strangers. « Rescue them ‹ from the mire ‹ so that they not sink; « may they be saved ‹ from the roaring [waves] ‹

וּמִמַּעֲמַקֵּי יָם.[3] וּבְנֵי יִשְׂרָאֵל הַהוֹלְכִים בַּיַּבָּשָׁה, הַדְרִיכֵם

and from the depths ‹ of the ocean. « As for the members of Israel ‹ who travel ‹ over land « lead them — ‹

בְּדֶרֶךְ יְשָׁרָה* לָלֶכֶת אֶל עִיר מוֹשָׁב,[4] וְתַצִּילֵם מִכַּף

on a path ‹ that is straight,* « to go ‹ to ‹ a city ‹ that is inhabited. « Rescue them ‹ from the hand ‹

כָּל אוֹיֵב וְאוֹרֵב בַּדֶּרֶךְ.[5] וְכָל הָאֲסוּרִים בְּכֶלֶא מֵעַמְּךָ

of every ‹ enemy ‹ or ambusher ‹ along the way. « As for all ‹ those incarcerated ‹ in prison ‹ from among ‹

יִשְׂרָאֵל, הַתֵּר מַאֲסָרֵיהֶם וְתוֹצִיאֵם לִרְוָחָה, וְהָשֵׁב

Israel « release [them from] — ‹ their imprisonment, « and bring them out ‹ to expansive freedom. « Restore ‹

לְיִרְאָתְךָ כָּל הָאֲנוּסִים בְּיַד גֵּאִים, וְתָחֹן זְכוּת אָבוֹת

to reverence of You ‹ all ‹ who were coerced [to convert] ‹ at the hands ‹ of the haughty. « Recall graciously ‹ the merit ‹ of our forefathers, «

לְהוֹצִיא לָאוֹר מִשְׁפָּטֵנוּ, כָּתְבֵנוּ בְּסֵפֶר חַיִּים, לְמַעַנְךָ

and bring out ‹ to light ‹ our verdict. « Inscribe us ‹ in the Book ‹ of Life « for Your sake, — ‹

אֱלֹהִים חַיִּים,[6] וְהָאֵר פָּנֶיךָ עַל מִקְדָּשְׁךָ הַשָּׁמֵם

O living God. « Shine ‹ Your countenance ‹ upon ‹ Your Sanctuary, ‹ which is desolate, ‹

לְמַעַן אֲדֹנָי.[7]

for the sake ‹ of my Lord. «

(1) Cf. *Psalms* 107:23. (2) Cf. 144:7. (3) Cf. 69:15. (4) Cf. 107:4. (5) Wayfarer's Prayer.
(6) Addition to *Shemoneh Esrei* during Days of Awe. (7) *Daniel* 9:17.

הַהוֹלְכִים בַּיַּבָּשָׁה, הַדְרִיכֵם בְּדֶרֶךְ יְשָׁרָה — *Who travel over land — lead them on a path that is straight.* The traveler requires Divine assistance to negotiate these difficult passages and obstacles.

As *Sifri* (*Deuteronomy* 20) states: There is no road that does not have crooked parts; there is no road that does not have pitfalls; there is no road that does not have forks and crossroads.

אֱלֹהֵינוּ וֵאלֹהֵי אֲבוֹתֵינוּ, מֶלֶךְ רַחֲמָן, רַחֵם עָלֵינוּ,*

« Our God 〈 and the God 〈 of our forefathers, « O King 〈 Who is merciful, 〈 have mercy 〈 on us;* «

טוֹב וּמֵטִיב* הִדָּרֶשׁ לָנוּ, שׁוּבָה אֵלֵינוּ* בַּהֲמוֹן רַחֲמֶיךָ,[1]

〈 O good 〈 and beneficent One,* 〈 let Yourself be sought out by us. « Return 〈 to us* 〈 in the yearning 〈 of Your mercy, «

בִּגְלַל אָבוֹת שֶׁעָשׂוּ רְצוֹנֶךָ.* בְּנֵה בֵיתְךָ כְּבַתְּחִלָּה,*

〈 for the sake 〈 of the Patriarchs 〈 who did « Your will.* 〈 Rebuild 〈 Your House 〈 as it was at first,* «

(1) Cf. *Isaiah* 63:15.

אֱלֹהֵינוּ וֵאלֹהֵי אֲבוֹתֵינוּ / Our God and the God of our forefathers

מֶלֶךְ רַחֲמָן רַחֵם עָלֵינוּ — *O King Who is Merciful, have mercy on us.* This section is taken from the Mussaf *Shemoneh Esrei* service of שָׁלֹשׁ רְגָלִים, *the three pilgrimage festivals.* Since the service of the festivals formerly centered around the Temple, the loss of that holiest of structures is most keenly felt during our festival celebrations. This supplication gives voice to Israel's yearning to see the Temple rebuilt.

A great question arises as to whether God will rebuild the Temple with His מִדַּת הָרַחֲמִים, *Attribute of Mercy,* or with His מִדַּת הַדִּין, *Attribute of Strict Justice.*

טוֹב וּמֵטִיב — *O good and beneficent One.* This is based on *Psalms* 119:68, טוֹב אַתָּה וּמֵטִיב, *good are You, and beneficent.* You are *good* even when You are not asked for kindness, and *beneficent* to those who request it (*Metzudas David*).

Iyun Tefillah observes that some people are good-hearted by nature, but lack the means to be beneficent to others. Other people are hard-hearted by nature, yet they force themselves to be beneficent to others in order to fulfill the demands and precepts of the Torah. But the Almighty is both innately *good* and superbly endowed with the means to be *beneficent* to all.

שׁוּבָה אֵלֵינוּ — *Return to us.* As the prophet says (*Malachi* 3 :7): שׁוּבוּ אֵלַי וְאָשׁוּבָה אֲלֵיכֶם, *Return to Me, and I will return to You.* The ה, *hei,* appended to שׁוּב, *return,* denotes intense desire (*Iyun Tefillah*). Also, it alludes to the verse (*Isaiah* 30:15): בְּשׁוּבָה וָנַחַת תִּוָּשֵׁעוּן, *with tranquility and ease you will be saved* (*Eitz Yoseif*).

בִּגְלַל אָבוֹת שֶׁעָשׂוּ רְצוֹנֶךָ — *For the sake of the Patriarchs who did Your will.* Scripture assured Israel, *For a God of mercy is Hashem, Your God, He will not loosen His grip on you, neither will He destroy you, and He will not forget the covenant of your fathers, that which He promised to them* (*Deuteronomy* 4:31).

In *Leviticus* (Ch. 26), Scripture provides a detailed description of the calamities and devastation that will befall the Jewish people if they abandon God and betray His covenant. Nevertheless, even after Israel's treachery, God reiterates His promise, *And I shall remember My covenant with Jacob, and even my covenant with Isaac, and even my covenant with Abraham I shall remember, and I shall remember the land* (ibid. v. 43).[1]

בְּנֵה בֵיתְךָ כְּבַתְּחִלָּה — *Rebuild Your House as it was at first.* The Midrash (*Bereishis Rabbah* 13:2) says that Israel's prayers still center

1. The commentators observe that God is obligated, as it were, to preserve the existence of Israel for two reasons: (1) זְכוּת אָבוֹת, the merits of the Patriarchs, who fulfilled His every demand and always adhered to His will. (2) בְּרִית אָבוֹת, the covenant God made with the Patriarchs.

Some commentators maintain that the merit of the Patriarchs endured only as long as their descendants followed their example and adhered to God's will. When Israel forsook God's ways, He abandoned them and "forgot" the merits of their forebears. Thus, according to this view, only the eternal inviolable covenant of the Patriarchs survives to protect Israel [see *Shabbos* 55a and *Tosafos* s.v. שְׁמוּאֵל אָמַר תַּמָּה זְכוּת אָבוֹת].

Iyun Tefillah notes that this liturgical passage supports the view that the merit of the Patriarchs endures because we implore God to redeem us not merely because of the covenant but also *for the sake of the Patriarchs who did Your will.*

וְכוֹנֵן בֵּית מִקְדָּשְׁךָ עַל מְכוֹנוֹ, וְהַרְאֵנוּ בְּבִנְיָנוֹ, וְשַׂמְּחֵנוּ

‹ and establish ‹ Your Sanctuary ‹ on ‹ its prepared site; « show us ‹ its rebuilding ‹ and gladden us

בְּתִקּוּנוֹ,* וְהָשֵׁב שְׁכִינָתְךָ לְתוֹכוֹ, וְהָשֵׁב כֹּהֲנִים לַעֲבוֹדָתָם

in its restoration.* « Restore ‹ Your *Shechinah* ‹ to its midst; « restore ‹ the Kohanim ‹ to their service «

וּלְוִיִּם לְדוּכָנָם, לְשִׁירָם וּלְזִמְרָם, וְהָשֵׁב יִשְׂרָאֵל לִנְוֵיהֶם.[1]

and the Levites ‹ to their platform, ‹ to their song ‹ and their music; « and restore ‹ Israel ‹ to their dwellings. «

וּמָלְאָה הָאָרֶץ דֵּעָה אֶת יהוה[2] לְיִרְאָה וּלְאַהֲבָה

And may ‹ the earth be filled ‹ with knowledge ‹ of ‹ HASHEM, « to fear ‹ and to love ‹

אֶת שִׁמְךָ הַגָּדוֹל וְהַנּוֹרָא. אָמֵן, כֵּן יְהִי רָצוֹן.

Your Name, ‹ which is great, ‹ and awesome. « Amen. « May such ‹ be ‹ Your will. «

(1) *Mussaf* for the Three Festivals. (2) Cf. *Isaiah* 11:9.

on the reconstruction of the Temple: "Master, rebuild the Temple! Master, rebuild the *Beis HaMikdash!'*

The *Yerushalmi* (*Yoma* 1:1) condemns Israel for failing in their prayers: Every generation for whom the *Beis HaMikdash* is not rebuilt is considered as if it caused its destruction.

The prayer is that God, *Himself*, rebuild it.

The first and second Temples were built by human hands; the third one, however, will be built by the hands of the Almighty Himself (*Rashi, Succah* 41a, *Rosh Hashanah* 30a; *Tosafos, Shevuos* 15b).

Rambam, however, appears to have a different opinion. He emphasizes that the king Messiah will be the one to rebuild the *Beis HaMikdash* and gather in the exiles of Israel (*Hilchos Melachim* 11:1,4).

Some commentators explain that if Israel's fervent prayers and fulfillment of the precepts merit that the date of redemption be hastened (אֲחִישֶׁנָּה), then the Temple will descend from heaven immediately in fiery form. But if Israel fails to generate enthusiasm and fiery yearning for the Temple, then the redemption will have to wait for its preordained time (בְּעִתּוֹ). In the latter course of events, reconstruction will follow a natural course, through the hands of men, under the direction of the Messiah.

וְהַרְאֵנוּ בְּבִנְיָנוֹ, וְשַׂמְּחֵנוּ בְּתִקּוּנוֹ — *Show us its rebuilding, and gladden us in its restoration.*

Maharil Diskin interpreted this passage in light of the verse: טָבְעוּ בָאָרֶץ שְׁעָרֶיהָ, *Her gates sunk into the earth* (*Lamentations* 2:9). Although the *Beis HaMikdash* was destroyed, it is destined to be completely rebuilt; why, then, were its gates swallowed by the earth, rather than destroyed?

The third *Beis HaMikdash* will be rebuilt by God in fire. When the Jews behold this wondrous edifice, their joy will be tinged with sorrow and disappointment because they will be deprived of the opportunity to participate in the reconstruction.

Therefore, God preserved intact the original gates that had been built by Israel. He will permit the Jews to attach these gates to the fiery edifice. The Talmud *(Bava Basra* 52b) rules that the person who puts up protective gates on a house is considered as if he built the entire house. Thus, after the Jews *behold the rebuilding* by God of the Sanctuary, they will *rejoice in* its *completion*, when they put up its gates (*Siddur HaGra; Siach Yitzchak*).

כָּל כְּלִי* יוּצַר עָלַיִךְ לֹא יִצְלָח, וְכָל לָשׁוֹן תָּקוּם

‹ Any ‹ weapon* ‹ sharpened ‹ against you ‹ will not « succeed, ‹ and any ‹ tongue ‹ that will rise

אִתָּךְ לַמִּשְׁפָּט תַּרְשִׁיעִי, זֹאת נַחֲלַת* עַבְדֵי יהוה

‹ against you ‹ in judgment « you will condemn. ‹ This ‹ is the heritage* ‹ of the servants ‹ of HASHEM

וְצִדְקָתָם מֵאִתִּי, נְאֻם יהוה.[1]

‹ and their righteousness « from Me ‹ – the word « of HASHEM.

לֹא יָרֵעוּ* וְלֹא יַשְׁחִיתוּ* בְּכָל הַר קָדְשִׁי,* כִּי

‹ They will not ‹ injure* ‹ nor ‹ will they destroy* ‹ in all « of My sacred mountain,* ‹ for

(1) *Isaiah* 54:17.

כְּלִי — *Any weapon.* This verse concludes one of Isaiah's prophecies of Israel's eventual redemption and triumph. He assures them that none of their enemies will succeed in inflicting either physical or verbal violence upon Jews.

זֹאת נַחֲלַת — *This is the heritage.* The above blessing remains the eternal heritage of the Jewish people (*Radak*).

לֹא יָרֵעוּ — *They will not injure* [lit., *they accomplish no evil*]. *Malbim* differentiates between the terms מֵרִיעַ and מַשְׁחִית, both of which refer to one who causes injury. The מֵרִיעַ is *one who injures* for his own benefit or pleasure, but the מַשְׁחִית is *one who destroys* and gains nothing from the damage he inflicts. The latter is driven solely by the desire to destroy.

[The prophet foretells an era of tranquility and peace. Then harmony and brotherhood will reign and even the most hostile and malicious creature will be tame and amiable.]

Prior to this, the prophet foretold: *The wolf shall dwell with the sheep, the leopard shall lay down with the kid, and the calf, lion and cub, and fatted cow will be together (Isaiah* 11 :6).

Radak explains that in the Messianic era carnivorous animals will revert to the herbivorous diet that they had maintained before Adam's sin.

Leviticus 26:6 contains the Divine promise, *And I will eradicate the evil beasts from the earth. Ramban* quotes two opinions cited in the Midrash: R' Yehudah interprets this verse literally and contends that the wild beast will actually be wiped out; R' Shimon, however, maintains that only the *hostile nature* of these creatures will disappear. *Ramban* prefers the second opinion; he explains that there were no predators in the world before Adam sinned. Only after man introduced evil into the world did evil become ingrained into the nature of certain beasts.

וְלֹא יַשְׁחִיתוּ — *Nor will they destroy.* In the preceding verse (11:8), Isaiah foresees a dramatic transformation in the behavior of the most vicious creatures: *The suckling babe shall play on the scorpion's pit, and the weaned child shall place his hand over the viper's nest.* Ordinarily snakes are מַשְׁחִית they *destroy* without deriving any pleasure from their prey. This vicious, lethal urge will be tamed in the epoch of the Messiah (*Malbim*).

בְּכָל הַר קָדְשִׁי — *In all of My sacred mountain.* The Mishnah (*Avos* 5:7) relates that ten miracles were wrought for our forefathers in the Temple. One of these miracles was that a serpent or scorpion never injured anyone in Jerusalem.

Tosefos Yom Tov observes that the Mishnah does not say that no snake ever *bit* anyone in Jerusalem. That would not necessarily indicate miraculous protection, for perhaps everyone took precautions to stay a safe distance from these deadly creatures. He explains that the

מָלְאָה הָאָרֶץ דֵּעָה אֶת יהוה, כַּמַּיִם לַיָּם מְכַסִּים.*[1]

« covers the seabed.* ‹ as water « HASHEM, ‹ of ‹ with knowledge ‹ will the earth be ‹ filled

(1) *Isaiah* 11:9.

miracle was that even though people *did* suffer occasional snake bites in Jerusalem, no one ever died as a result of these injuries.

Midrash Shmuel and *Tiferes Yisrael* (*Avos* 5:7) note that this phenomenon persists to this very day. Although the Temple lies in ruins, the sanctity of the Temple endures and counteracts the poison of the snakes.

Based on this, we can explain the words of Isaiah. In the past, the scorpions could not *kill* on the Temple Mount, but they could bite and injure. In the future, however, *they shall not injure nor destroy* in any way at all.

The benign, sacred atmosphere that emanates from *the sacred mountain* will spread throughout the world. The predominance of sanctity will generate an absence of sin, as the Talmud (*Berachos* 33a) states: It is not the serpent, but man's sin that causes death.

[The serpent is a symbol of sin because the very first creature to sin in the Garden of Eden was the serpent.]

כִּי מָלְאָה הָאָרֶץ דֵּעָה אֶת ה׳, כַּמַּיִם לַיָּם מְכַסִּים — *Filled will the earth be with knowledge of* HASHEM, *as water covers the sea.* Just as the sea is filled with water, the earth will be filled with the knowledge of God (*Metzudas David*).

At that time, God's Presence will be so apparent that even the wild beasts of prey will recognize Him. Even the dark earthiness of their nature will not obscure the infinite light of God's presence, just as nothing can restrain the power of the surging sea (*Malbim*).

Rambam (*Hilchos Melachim* 12:5) describes the future era of Messiah thus: At that time good things will be found in abundance; all luxuries will be as commonplace and available as dirt. Mankind will have no business nor concern other than the pursuit of the knowledge of God. Therefore, the Jewish people will be great sages who will comprehend matters hitherto regarded as incomprehensible. They will perceive the Divine intellect of their Creator, each and every one of them according to his own ability. As Scripture states, *the earth will be full of the knowledge of* HASHEM *as waters cover the sea.* [Compare with *Rambam, Hilchos Teshuvah* 9:2.]

Ohr Same'ach (*Hilchos Teshuvah* 9:2) notes that *Rambam* emphasizes that everyone will perceive Divine intellect *according to his own ability.* In This World, people often fail in their pursuit of wisdom because they study either beneath or above their levels. Their learning is impeded because it does not correspond to their actual capacity. In the future, however, everyone will learn according to his own ability.

This may be likened to the water that covers the sea floor with utmost precision. Every available space is filled with water, and the sea holds its full volume of water *according to its ability.*

R' Avraham Yitzchak Bloch quotes *Rambam* (*Hilchos Melachim* 12:1), who stresses that everything that happens in This World will continue in the future Messianic world; no extraordinary miracles will occur, no supernatural events will take place. If so, in what way will the future world be an improvement over the present one?

Actually, all "natural" events are wondrous Divine accomplishments. However, since they occur according to a predictable pattern, man fails to appreciate that these "natural" phenomena are Divine works. In the future, the processes of nature will not change; rather, a spirit of Divine wisdom will inspire man to perceive the Divine inner power that controls the world.

In this way, the future wisdom resembles the waters of the sea. The Talmud (*Chullin* 127a) states: Everything that is found on dry land can be found in the sea. The only reason that the marvels of the sea are not apparent to man is because they are covered by the waters. Similarly, the wonders of creation are not evident now because they are "cloaked," by the laws of nature, but Divine wisdom will reveal them all in the future.

שִׁיר לַמַּעֲלוֹת, אֶשָּׂא עֵינַי אֶל הֶהָרִים, מֵאַיִן יָבֹא

‹ will come ‹ from whence « the mountains; ‹ to ‹ my eyes ‹ I raise « to the ascents. ‹ A song

עֶזְרִי. עֶזְרִי מֵעִם יהוה, עֹשֵׂה שָׁמַיִם וָאָרֶץ.[1] וְאֹרַח

‹ The path « and earth. ‹ of heaven ‹ Maker « HASHEM, ‹ is from ‹ My help « my help?

צַדִּיקִים כְּאוֹר נֹגַהּ, הוֹלֵךְ וָאוֹר עַד נְכוֹן הַיּוֹם.[2] וַאֲנִי

« As for me, « of the day [noon]. ‹ the fullest part ‹ until ‹ growing brighter « that shines [at dawn], ‹ is like the light ‹ of the righteous

תְפִלָּתִי לְךָ יהוה עֵת רָצוֹן, אֱלֹהִים בְּרָב חַסְדֶּךָ, עֲנֵנִי

‹ answer me ‹ of Your kindness, ‹ in the abundance ‹ O God, « [be] at a time that is favorable; ‹ HASHEM, ‹ to You, ‹ may my prayer

בֶּאֱמֶת יִשְׁעֶךָ.[3] הִנֵּה לֹא יָנוּם וְלֹא יִישָׁן, שׁוֹמֵר יִשְׂרָאֵל.[4]

« of Israel. ‹ — the Guardian « sleeps ‹ nor ‹ [He] neither slumbers ‹ Behold, « of Your salvation. ‹ with the truth

הִנֵּה עֵין יהוה אֶל יְרֵאָיו, לַמְיַחֲלִים לְחַסְדּוֹ.[5] הוֹד וְהָדָר

‹ and splendor ‹ Majesty « His kindness. ‹ upon those who await « those who fear Him, ‹ is on ‹ of HASHEM ‹ the eye ‹ Behold,

לְפָנָיו, עֹז וְחֶדְוָה בִּמְקֹמוֹ.[6] כִּי עִמְּךָ הַסְּלִיחָה, לְמַעַן

‹ so that « is forgiveness, ‹ with You ‹ For « are in His place. ‹ and delight ‹ might « are before Him,

תִּוָּרֵא.[7] רַחוּם וְחַנּוּן יהוה, אֶרֶךְ אַפַּיִם וְרַב חָסֶד.[8] בְּאוֹר

‹ In the light « and Abundant of Kindness. ‹ to Anger ‹ Slow « is HASHEM, ‹ and Gracious ‹ Compassionate « You may be feared.

פְּנֵי מֶלֶךְ חַיִּים, וּרְצוֹנוֹ כְּעָב מַלְקוֹשׁ.[9] כִּי אֵל גָּדוֹל

‹ a great God ‹ For « [bringing] rain. ‹ is like a cloud ‹ and his favor « is life, ‹ of the countenance of the king

יהוה, וּמֶלֶךְ גָּדוֹל עַל כָּל אֱלֹהִים.[10] אַשְׁרֵי הָעָם יוֹדְעֵי

‹ who know ‹ is the people ‹ Praiseworthy « heavenly powers. ‹ all ‹ above ‹ and a great King « is HASHEM,

תְרוּעָה, יהוה בְּאוֹר פָּנֶיךָ יְהַלֵּכוּן.[11] כַּשֶּׁמֶן הַטּוֹב עַל הָרֹאשׁ,

‹ the head, ‹ upon ‹ that is superior ‹ Like the oil « they walk. ‹ by the illumination of Your countenance ‹ HASHEM, « the shofar's cry;

יֹרֵד עַל הַזָּקָן, זְקַן אַהֲרֹן, שֶׁיֹּרֵד עַל פִּי מִדּוֹתָיו.[12]

« his garments. ‹ over ‹ running down « of Aaron, ‹ the beard « the beard, ‹ upon ‹ running down

(1) *Psalms* 121:1-2. (2) *Proverbs* 4:18. (3) *Psalms* 69:14. (4) 121:4. (5) 33:18. (6) *I Chronicles* 16:27. (7) *Psalms* 130:4. (8) 103:8. (9) *Proverbs* 16:15. (10) *Psalms* 95:3. (11) 89:16. (12) 133:2.

יְהִי רָצוֹן מִלְּפָנֶיךָ, שֶׁעַל יְדֵי הֶאָרַת תִּקּוּנִים עַתִּיקָא

May it be ‹ the will ‹ before You « that by ‹ means ‹ of the illuminating ‹ perfections ‹ of the Ancient ‹

קַדִּישָׁא דְעַתִּיקִין בִּזְעֵיר שֶׁבְּאָרִיךְ, יִכְבְּשׁוּ רַחֲמֶיךָ

Holy One, ‹ which are eternal ‹ in the microcosm ‹ of infinitude, ‹ that suppress ‹ may Your mercy ‹

אֶת כַּעַסְךָ, וְיָגֹלּוּ רַחֲמֶיךָ עַל מִדּוֹתֶיךָ,* וְתִתְנַהֵג עִמָּנוּ בְּמִדַּת

Your anger, « and overwhelm ‹ may Your mercy ‹ Your Attributes. « May You conduct Yourself ‹ with us ‹ with the Attribute ‹

הָרַחֲמִים, וְתִתֶּן לָנוּ חַיִּים אֲרוּכִים וְטוֹבִים בְּעִסְקֵי תוֹרָתֶךָ

of Mercy, « and grant ‹ us ‹ a life ‹ that is long ‹ and good, « with involvement ‹ in [the study of] Your Torah ‹

וְקִיּוּם מִצְוֹתֶיךָ, לַעֲשׂוֹת רְצוֹנְךָ, אָמֵן, כֵּן יְהִי רָצוֹן.

and observance ‹ of Your commandments, « [in order that we] perform ‹ Your will. « Amen, « may ‹ such ‹ be ‹ Your will. «

Psalm 130 — תהלים קל

שִׁיר הַמַּעֲלוֹת;* מִמַּעֲמַקִּים קְרָאתִיךָ, יהוה. אֲדֹנָי,

A song ‹ of ascents.* « From the depths ‹ I called You, ‹ HASHEM. « O Lord, ‹

שִׁמְעָה בְקוֹלִי, תִּהְיֶינָה אָזְנֶיךָ קַשֻּׁבוֹת לְקוֹל תַּחֲנוּנָי. אִם

hear ‹ my voice; « may they be « — Your ears — « attentive ‹ to the sound ‹ of my pleas. « If ‹

עֲוֹנוֹת תִּשְׁמָר, יָהּ, אֲדֹנָי, מִי יַעֲמֹד. כִּי עִמְּךָ הַסְּלִיחָה,

iniquities ‹ You preserve, ‹ O God, « O Lord, ‹ who ‹ could survive? « For ‹ with You ‹ is forgiveness, «

לְמַעַן תִּוָּרֵא. קִוִּיתִי יהוה, קִוְּתָה נַפְשִׁי, וְלִדְבָרוֹ הוֹחָלְתִּי.

so that ‹ You may be feared. « I placed my hope ‹ in HASHEM, « placed hope ‹ did my soul, « and for His word ‹ I yearned. «

שיר המעלות / A Song of Ascents

The New Year commences. The Jew has repented and shed his burden of bygone sins, but what has he done to rid himself of the factors that *caused* him to sin? Who can fathom the source of sin, the deep and complex emotions that lead man toward error and transgression? True inner purity cannot be attained without inner searching and cleansing.

Rambam places great emphasis on this point in the final words of *Hilchos Mikvaos* (11:12): The man who immerses himself in the waters of ritual purification rids himself of his contamination even though he has surely not made any significant physical changes in his body. Similarly, one who concentrates on cleansing himself of evil thoughts and sinful ideas, in effect immerses his soul in the waters of pure wisdom.

The Midrash (*Vayikra Rabbah* 3:7) stresses that only a deep and comprehensive knowledge of Torah can penetrate the depths of man, overcoming his dark passions and enlightening his troubled spirit. King Solomon

נַפְשִׁי לַאדֹנָי, מִשֹּׁמְרִים לַבֹּקֶר, שֹׁמְרִים לַבֹּקֶר. יַחֵל

〈 My soul 〈〈 [yearns] for the Lord, 〈 among those longing 〈〈 for the dawn 〈 those longing 〈〈 for the dawn 〈 Yearn

יִשְׂרָאֵל אֶל יהוה; כִּי עִם יהוה הַחֶסֶד, וְהַרְבֵּה עִמּוֹ

〈 shall Israel 〈 for 〈〈 HASHEM, 〈 for 〈 with 〈 HASHEM 〈〈 is kindness, 〈 and abundant 〈 with Him

פְדוּת. וְהוּא יִפְדֶּה אֶת יִשְׂרָאֵל, מִכֹּל עֲוֹנוֹתָיו.

〈〈 is redemption. 〈 And He 〈 shall redeem 〈 Israel 〈 from all 〈 its iniquities. 〈〈

RECITE SEVEN TIMES:

לְעוֹלָם יהוה דְּבָרְךָ נִצָּב בַּשָּׁמָיִם.[1] *

〈 Forever, 〈 HASHEM, 〈 Your word 〈 stands firm 〈〈 in the heavens.*

(1) *Psalms* 119:89.

said (*Proverbs* 20:5): מַיִם עֲמֻקִּים עֵצָה בְלֶב־אִישׁ וְאִישׁ תְּבוּנָה יִדְלֶנָּה, *Counsel in the heart of man is like deep water, but a man of understanding will draw it up.* Therefore, concludes the Midrash, when David composed *A Song of Ascents*, he began, *From the depths I called You, Hashem;* he intended to ascend from the grip of sin, and his way of doing so was by climbing the rungs of Torah.

⊱ לְעוֹלָם ה׳ דְּבָרְךָ נִצָּב בַּשָּׁמָיִם / Forever, Hashem, Your word stands firm in the heavens.

At the time of Creation You said but a word, and a firmament appeared in the heavens! This accomplishment endures לְעוֹלָם, *forever*, for the stars and the celestial legions *stand firm* for all time (*Radak*).

Alshich observes that when a mortal utters a word, it immediately vanishes into thin air. The word of God, however, emanates in a holy fire that is not consumed or dissipated. Elsewhere (*Psalms* 33:6) the psalmist declares: *By the word of HASHEM the heavens were made, and by the breath of His mouth all their host.* God's breath is part of Him. Just as He is eternal, so is His breath and His word.

Similarly, Isaiah (40:8) says: *The grass withers, the flower fades, but the word of our God shall stand forever* (*Midrash Shocher Tov*).

Moreover, *Pesikta Rabbasi* (40) derives from the use in our verse of the Four-Letter Name, that it is as the Dispenser of Mercy that Hashem stands firm forever, even when He sits in judgment and exercises His Attribute of Strict Justice.

This has been the case since the very dawn of Creation. The universe was created on the twenty-fifth day of Elul. Six days later, on the first of Tishrei, Adam was brought forth from the earth. On that very day he sinned. Although God was filled with wrath, He did not destroy Adam, because He tempered His anger with the Attribute of "Hashem," Dispenser of Mercy.

Hashem *stands firm* in His practice of exercising mercy לְעוֹלָם, *forever*. Thus he displays it every year, on the first of Tishrei, which He ordained as Rosh Hashanah, the day when all creatures pass in judgment before Him.